UNCONSCIOUS SCORING

Also by Dave Stockton

UNCONSCIOUS PUTTING

UNCONSCIOUS SCORING

Dave Stockton's Guide to Saving
Shots Around the Green

DAVE STOCKTON
with Matthew Rudy

GOTHAM BOOKS

GOTHAM BOOKS
Published by Penguin Group (USA) Inc.
375 Hudson Street, New York, New York 10014, U.S.A.
Penguin Group (Canada), 90 Eglinton Avenue East, Suite 700, Toronto, Ontario M4P 2Y3, Canada
(a division of Pearson Penguin Canada Inc.); Penguin Books Ltd, 80 Strand, London WC2R 0RL,
England; Penguin Ireland, 25 St Stephen's Green, Dublin 2, Ireland (a division of Penguin Books
Ltd); Penguin Group (Australia), 250 Camberwell Road, Camberwell, Victoria 3124, Australia
(a division of Pearson Australia Group Pty Ltd); Penguin Books India Pvt Ltd, 11 Community
Centre, Panchsheel Park, New Delhi–110 017, India; Penguin Group (NZ), 67 Apollo Drive,
Rosedale, Auckland 0632, New Zealand (a division of Pearson New Zealand Ltd); Penguin Books
(South Africa) (Pty) Ltd, 24 Sturdee Avenue, Rosebank, Johannesburg 2196, South Africa

Penguin Books Ltd, Registered Offices: 80 Strand, London WC2R 0RL, England

Published by Gotham Books, a member of Penguin Group (USA) Inc.

First printing, September 2012
10 9 8 7 6 5 4 3 2 1

LIBRARY OF CONGRESS CATALOGING-IN-PUBLICATION DATA

Stockton, Dave.
   Unconscious scoring : Dave Stockton's guide to saving shots around the green / Dave Stockton
with Matthew Rudy.
      p.   cm.
   ISBN 978-1-592-40776-7
   1. Golf—Training.   I. Rudy, Matthew.   II. Title.
   GV979.T68S86   2012
   796.352'3—dc23   2012018756

Printed in the United States of America
Set in 11pt. Berkeley Oldstyle
Designed by Julie Schroeder
Unless otherwise noted, all photos are courtesy of J. D. Cuban

While the author has made every effort to provide accurate telephone numbers, Internet
addresses, and other contact information at the time of publication, neither the publisher nor the
author assumes any responsibility for errors, or for changes that occur after publication. Further,
the publisher does not have any control over and does not assume any responsibility for author or
third-party websites or their content.

CONTENTS

Foreword by Rory McIlroy   vii

Preface by Lee Trevino   ix

Introduction   xi

Chapters

   One   The Essence of Scoring   1

   Two   Increasing Your Short-game Awareness   9

   Three Low Shots   16

   Four   High Shots   28

   Five   Bunkers   39

   Six   Trouble Shots   54

   Seven Mental Game   71

   Eight Practice and Drills   78

   Nine   Equipment   97

   Ten   Putting   107

Acknowledgments   125

FOREWORD

By Rory McIlroy

Back in the middle of 2010, my caddie, J. P. Fitzgerald, suggested that I get together with Dave Stockton to work on my putting. At the time, I was happy to do my own thing, so I left it alone for a while. But after the tough finish at the Masters in 2011, I felt like there were some things I needed to address. I read some things Dave had to say about putting and the short game, and I knew that he was very into feel and keeping things natural with your stroke.

I figured that was a great place to start. My game is based on feel, and I didn't think my putting matched the rest of it. It seemed like it would be a good fit.

Dave and I got together at the event in Charlotte, and the first thing we did was sit down and talk for half an hour. If you've read Dave's last book, *Unconscious Putting*, you know what we did first. He asked me to write my signature on a piece of paper, and then he asked me to do it much slower, as if I was tracing it. Then he asked me which way I thought it would be easier to putt—in a natural, subconscious way or a controlled, conscious way. That really hit me, and showed me that my putting needed to be in-line with the rest of my game—based on instinct and feel. It took me fifteen minutes, max, to get it, and we've been working on many of the same things since. I pick my target, pick the spot on my line, let it go, and roll the ball over my spot, trying to get the back of my left hand to go toward the hole. It was incredibly freeing to have such a simple routine to follow. It uncluttered my mind, and gave me something I could count on, whether I'm on the first green on Thursday morning or the seventy-second hole on Sunday afternoon.

Obviously, after the way this last year has turned out, we're still going strong. If it wasn't for Dave, I don't know if I could have gone on this run, winning the U.S. Open and reaching the top of the world rankings. With Dave, it's simple. I've made more putts and shot lower scores, and you can see it in my results.

Most of our work comes on putting, but I can see how much sense Dave's ideas work in the short game as well. I play a lot of practice rounds with 15- or 20-handicappers, and I see them standing over a chip shot or a bunker shot, just paralyzed. You wonder what they're thinking about. They're overwhelmed by so many mechanical thoughts that they don't know where to start.

If that sounds familiar, take a step back and let Dave help you simplify your approach, improve your technique, and clear your mind. To me, nobody has more authority on the subject of putting and short game. Dave is a multiple major championship winner and a Ryder Cup captain, and these lessons mean more coming from someone who has been through it himself as a player. He knew that he had to hit better short-game shots and make more putts than the other guys to win tournaments, and he did it. You can also see from the first day how positive he is, and how much he really cares. He takes pride in the results his students post, whether they come at a major championship or a local amateur event.

He shows you how to be a better player and puts you in the right mindset to go out and do it. I don't believe there's any more you could ask from a teacher.

Rory McIlroy
Holywood, Northern Ireland
April 30, 2012

PREFACE

By Lee Trevino

The first I ever really saw of Dave Stockton was in 1967, when he was just a couple of years out onto the PGA Tour. All the guys who won the Colonial National Invitation in Dallas got a vote for two non-exempt players to invite, and Dave was one of them. At the Masters or the U.S. Open, you won by driving the ball. At Colonial, you needed to be a magician around those small greens and all the bunkers. It was a perfect place for Dave, and he ended up winning the tournament that first year we invited him.

I always say that Dave's father must have been a genius. Dave wasn't the longest hitter, or even the straightest, but I bet his dad knew that if Dave was ever going to make his living at this game, he was going to have to know how to play from 100 yards and in.

That's something I'm familiar with, because I came up the same way. I grew up playing a par-3 course with one club, and I had to learn how to hit a lot of different shots. I wasn't born with that talent with my wedges, but I earned it, and so did Dave. I got to be great with the wedge because I had to, and so did Dave. He and I proved that you don't have to be 6-foot-4 and hit it 320 yards to win. I put him right up there with the greatest short-game players I've ever seen—Seve Ballesteros, Hubert Green, Raymond Floyd. And he's obviously one of the greatest putters ever, right there with Ben Crenshaw and Jack Nicklaus. And those skills have never left him, like they have for some other players.

Where we're different is that Dave knows what's behind it, and he can show you how to do it the same way every time—both on the green and around it. Dave learned the game when you had one wedge to hit every short-game shot, and he knows how to explain the mechanics and feel to you. I did it a lot of different, crazy ways, and changed all the time. I knew what I was doing, but I didn't know so much about how to get you to play better.

Now players have so many different wedges in their bag, and they're stuck when they get to a shot that doesn't fit into a simple box. They never give themselves the chance to be great by developing that touch and feel. If I was a young guy playing golf today, the first thing I'd do is seek out Dave and his sons to teach me how to putt and how to hit short-game shots. Until you know how to play those, you don't really know how to play. You don't live with the driver and the approach shots. You live with the short game, and it's the only way your game is ever going to travel. You're not going to hit every green. You're going to get into some tough spots, and you're going to be in some bunkers.

We used to see all kinds of guys who learned the few shots they needed at their own course, but when they went someplace else, they couldn't play. We'd joke and tell them not to take their game out of town, because they couldn't get parts for it. There's even some of that on the tour right now.

My son is a young player now, in his freshman year of college, and he and I are taking a tour this year to play all the different kinds of courses. He's a good player, but he's still learning how to play the game. An important part of his training is learning those short finesse shots that make your game travel, like the shots you're going to learn in this book. If you have any aspirations to be a good player—whether you're an amateur or a pro—you need to go see the Stocktons, or at least listen to what they have to say here.

You'll find all the parts you need.

Lee Trevino
Dallas, Texas
March 27, 2012

INTRODUCTION

Fear.

That's the main emotion a lot of players feel when they're standing in the fairway, getting ready to hit an approach shot. Call it anxiety, or indecision, or worry, or whatever you like, but fear is the basic emotion that rules so many players' golf lives.

And it isn't because they don't know where their 7-iron or 9-iron is going to go—although that can be a little part of it.

Mainly, it's because they're worried about the ball going in the bunker, or ending up in deep grass around the green, or even in a place where they have to hit a chip shot. And if they putt like many amateur players do, hitting it on the green isn't a solution, either, because they're worried about being in three-putt territory.

Even a small amount of fear or doubt puts a lot of pressure on your game, and it makes it very difficult to stand over a shot and make a loose, free swing. Fear and pressure make the game less fun, and they make your scores go up.

What if you could make some simple changes to your mental approach and technique and transform your short game from something to fear into something you look forward to doing? Imagine standing over your approach shot completely focused on the positive—where you want it to go—because you're not particularly worried about what will happen if it goes someplace you don't want.

Imagine getting into the bunker and looking forward to hitting what I think is the easiest shot in golf. Or walking up to your ball just off the green and having the tools to read the situation and pick one of two simple short-game shots to get you closer to the hole—or even make it.

If you read my last book, *Unconscious Putting*, you know that I believe—and can prove—that putting is an art form that any player can learn. There's no magic to it, or any steep learning curve of technical information that has to be mastered in order to do it well. In the short game, there are a few more mechanical basics to learn, but the overall premise is exactly the same. If you can learn how to think better before each shot and to perform two simple swings, you can have an excellent short game in less time than it will take you to read this book.

How do I know that?

The proof is in the results that my two sons and I have seen at the hundreds of short-game clinics and schools we've taught over the last twenty years. And it's reinforced by the successful—and brief—lessons we've taught to tour players from around the world. We've seen 20-handicap business-people turn into 10-handicappers in the space of a few months, and we've helped multiple major-championship winners go from average in tour short-game statistics to the top of the class.

Just like in putting, there is a lot of information on the short game out there. You can find a dozen books on the subject at your local bookstore, and multiple articles on it every month in *Golf Digest* and the other golf magazines. I'm not trying to say that any of that is bad information, or that the teachers sharing it are wrong. I just don't believe it has to be so complicated.

In *Unconscious Scoring*, I'm going to teach you the short game the same way I would if you came to one of our clinics. You'll learn how the short game flows from the putting stroke—from small, left-hand-dominant low shots to higher, right-hand-dominant ones. We'll also talk about how to see and pick different short-game shots, and how your mental pre-shot routine is just as important as your physical one.

Let me make one important point up front. If you haven't read my previous book, *Unconscious Putting*, go straight to the last chapter of this one, Chapter 10, where I give an overview on putting and explain some of the key points from that book. If you did read book one, you're still going to get a lot out of that chapter. I'll also touch on some mental game techniques I didn't talk about the first time, and talk about the explosion in popularity of belly putters on the professional tours. If you want to try one, I'm not going to stand in your way. I just want to give you the basics on how they work, and how to get the most out of them.

In Chapter 1, we're going to talk about the scoring mind-set, and what separates the players who get the most out of their game from those who seem to come up short a lot—whatever the handicap level. The simple fact is that more shots are taken from 50 yards and in than from any other place, so that's the area where improvement can make the most difference in your actual handicap number. The confidence level we talked about at the beginning of the introduction is the big mover. If you know you're better at shots around the green, your comfort level all the way back through your bag to the driver will improve, because you know you aren't doomed if you miss a shot.

Before you can actually hit any short-game shots, you have to be able to take a snapshot of your situation and pick the solution that has the best chance for success—and that feels the most comfortable to you. When I go through my routine before playing a chip or a pitch, I see in my mind a vivid image of exactly what my upcoming shot is going to do, from where it lands to how it bounces and where it ends up. That's not some magical talent that I was lucky to be born with. It's a learned skill, and one you can develop. In Chapter 2, I'll give you some techniques to do just that, and to greatly simplify the process of selecting the right shot to play in that situation.

We'll start to develop the tools you'll use to execute that short-game vision in Chapter 3. Once you've moved off the green, the first step is to learn how to hit a basic low chip shot. This low shot is controlled by the left hand just like a putt is, and is dead simple. Once you get comfortable with it, it will become your bread-and-butter shot on a good two-thirds of all your short-game situations. I'll show you how to subtly adjust your setup and ball position to change the distance the ball flies and rolls, and how to master hitting this shot with any club.

Once you know how to play low shots, we'll introduce high shots in Chapter 4. These you hit when you need to carry long grass or other trouble in front of you, or when you need to fly the ball onto a tier. A simple change in technique from the low shot turns this into a right-hand-dominated motion, and you'll be hitting high, soft shots in minutes.

The best part about the high shot technique you will learn is that it directly applies to the next shot on the schedule in Chapter 5—the bunker shot. Using the same right-hand-dominated swing and some slight adjustments to your footwork, you can gain control over your bunker play in a way you've never experienced. The basic bunker shot will go from being a sore spot to a shot you can't wait to hit.

Of course, not every shot is a plain, basic one from a perfect lie. In Chapter 6, we'll go through a variety of trouble shots from around the green and in the sand, and I'll show you how to play from hardpan, deep grass, bad bunker lies and awkward stances. You'll learn how to get back into position to save your score on a given hole.

I place just as much emphasis—if not more—on the mental side of the game as I do the physical, mechanical side. I don't believe you can become a good player unless you understand how the mind works, and how your thoughts and emotions affect your game. If you don't have positive, productive thoughts as a part of your pre-shot routine, any success you have will be almost by accident. In Chapter 7, we'll talk about building effective mental and physical pre-shot routines, and how to handle the successes and failures that are a part of the game.

On the physical side, it's also important to groove the feel of efficient, simple short-game shots. The best way to do that is to mix technique-specific drills with casual practice sessions that put an emphasis on experimentation. In Chapter 8, I'll give you a simple plan that you can use to practice the shots and techniques we talked about here. It's the same plan we've used to help dozens of tour players win at the highest level. With a few simple accessories like a tee and an adjustable target ring, you can build your own practice station and get the most out of your time. And you can go to my website, davestockton.com/scoringtips, to see videos of the lessons we talk about here.

In Chapter 9, we'll talk about picking the right equipment for your skill level and shot preference, and how physical factors like bounce and lie angle on a given wedge are just as particular and specific to the individual as the various measurements you'd take to get fit for a putter. There's a reason why you've hit wedges that just feel right, while others feel like a hunk of metal in your hands.

Chapter 10 is an introduction (or a refresher course) on where the short game starts—with the putter. The ultimate left-hand-dominated stroke, rolling your ball is more about seeing the line and quieting your mind than it is about mechanics. We'll talk about how to build sound mental and physical pre-shot routines, how to see and trust your read, and how to roll the ball on that line into the specific part of the hole that you've visualized. It might sound like a lot to bite off in about three thousand words, but I can tell you that dozens of tour players have won millions of dollars in part because of an hour-or-two lesson from Team Stockton. It's something that can and will click for the average player just as quickly and easily.

I got a lot of extremely nice compliments on *Unconscious Putting* after it came out, and hundreds of letters and e-mails from players who said it changed their putting game. I'm certainly thrilled I was able to help so many people, and I'm looking forward to doing the same thing here in *Unconscious Scoring*.

One of the great backhanded compliments that came out of the first book was that people wanted more. They may have enjoyed what we wrote, but they wanted more of it. I hate to say it, but anybody who takes more time than we did to describe how to roll the ball is probably making it more complicated than it needs to be.

I want to use the fewest words and the simplest techniques I can to help you play better. My mission is to get you to stop overthinking and start feeling and letting it go and enjoying yourself. I want golf to really be play, not work.

Like you've heard me say before, if you trust me—and trust the power of your unconscious mind—you'll be amazed at what you can do.

UNCONSCIOUS
SCORING

ONE

The Essence of Scoring

Watching the end of a professional tournament on Sunday afternoon, it's easy to see a simple definition of scoring. Look at the leaderboard, and the person at the top of it had the best week, shot the lowest number, and took home the trophy and the biggest check.

But if you asked that player—or any tour player—if "scoring" was mostly about hitting great shots and making birdies, he or she would say no. You need to hit those shots and make those putts to shoot a low number, but scoring is much more than that.

The truth is, we're all going to have good days and bad days. Sometimes, your swing just isn't what you want it to be. Or you don't feel great physically. Maybe you're distracted about something off the golf course. Or you're playing a new golf course and you don't like it that much.

Players who have a talent for scoring are able to get the most out of the game they have on any given day—or on any given hole. When they're feeling great and hitting great shots, they can make a great score—and I mean that relatively. If you're a 15-handicap and you go out and shoot 78, that's a great score. If you're Rory McIlroy or Phil Mickelson, I'm talking about a 63 or 64. And when they're off a little bit, understanding how to minimize risk and get out of trouble—specifically in the short game—turns a terrible day into a decent one. It can save a round or a tournament at the most crucial time.

Just think about some of the great short-game shots in recent tournament history and it's easy to see what I mean. Tiger Woods hit one of the most creative, clutch chip shots in history at the 16th hole at Augusta in the final round of the 2005 Masters. He hit his iron left of the green, and he was left with a shot that had almost 30 feet of break. He hit a low shot up above the hole, and then watched as it made a right turn, trickled down toward the hole, took another break to the left and then dropped into the cup on the last roll for a birdie. The stroke he saved there ended up being pretty important—he beat Chris DiMarco in a playoff to earn his fourth green jacket.

Tom Watson's chip-in from the deep grass next to the 17th green at Pebble Beach in the 1982 U.S. Open and Larry Mize's across-the-green chip-in at the 11th hole at Augusta to win his playoff against Greg Norman at the 1987 Masters are two other great examples of career-defining short-game shots that were the difference between victory and defeat. The ones that happen at the end of a round get all the attention—good and bad—but being able to extricate yourself from a difficult situation around the green on an early hole can change the entire complexion of the day. At the 2011 Masters, Charl Schwartzel missed the green on the first hole way right, in a spot where many players would have picked a flop shop. Instead, he picked a low pitch and run shot, holed it out, and was off to the races. Everybody will remember his four birdies in a row to finish the tournament—or even the shot he holed from the fairway on No. 3 for eagle—but it was the chip-in that kept him in the game. In all these cases, the lie dictated the shot that these guys picked—which we're going to talk about more in the next chapter.

I know how important the scoring clubs are, because I've lived it for almost 50 years, as both a player and teacher on the professional tours. I was never the longest or straightest hitter, and I was never the most consistent. But I was always able to compete and win at the highest level because I could extract good scores out of days when I wasn't hitting the ball that great from tee to green. I understood how to give myself the best chance to get up and down, and how to simplify the short game so that I could pick one of two kinds of shots to hit. Then, it was just a matter of committing to it and hitting the shot with a clear mind.

Many of my 24 wins on the PGA and Champions tours came down to crucial scoring shots from around and on the green. At the 1970 PGA at Southern Hills, I was leading the tournament after three rounds and paired with Arnold Palmer on Sunday. Arnie was at the absolute peak of his popularity. He had won all the majors at least once except the PGA, and his Army was out in full force rooting him on to complete the Grand Slam. On the 7th hole, I was getting ready to hit a wedge into the green, and somebody in the crowd yelled, "Shank it!" I holed that one out for eagle. And on 13, I hit my approach shot into the water and had an extremely difficult 40-yard pitch shot from the drop location, on pure hardpan. I could have thrown the tournament away there, but I hit my pitch to three inches to save an important bogey. I went on to win my first major by two shots over Arnold and Bob Murphy.

At the 1976 PGA at Congressional, I had a one-shot lead going to the 17th hole, and I hit my approach shot there into a deep bunker. The pin was on top of a severe ridge, with another ridge behind the tier. I had about three feet to land this shot without it either rolling back to my feet or away to a place where I'd have an extremely difficult putt. I hit the shot and the ball hit three inches short of the top of the slope, bounced forward about six inches and trickled up to tap-in range. I could have dropped twenty balls and not hit a better shot. I made the putt and went on to win my second PGA Championship.

I've been giving short-game and putting clinics for amateur players around the country for more than forty-five years, and I've been working with tour players for almost as long. When I was playing the tour, I helped players as much as I could when it didn't interfere with my playing—and as long as they promised not to tell anyone I was doing it. I worked with Tiger Woods on his short wedges just after he turned professional, in 1996, and with Annika Sorenstam on her putting in 1999—right before she won seventeen times in two years—among other players. I can tell you from those experiences that it wasn't some kind of magic that allowed me to hit all those shots and win all those tournaments. It was training I got, first from my dad and then from a handful of generous friends and co-competitors out on the tour. It's something anyone can learn. I've seen 20-handicap players come into a two-hour clinic unable to get a chip shot airborne and leave with the short game of a 10-handicapper. My sons and I have helped tour players go from the bottom 10 percent in the short game statistics to the top 10 percent in the course of a few lessons.

How?

You have to see the short game differently.

I learned how to play the game in the space between the 2nd and 11th greens at Arrowhead Country Club in San Bernardino, Calif. My dad, Gail, was the head professional there. At first, all I had was a 3-wood, a 6-iron, and a putter. Eventually, I got some wedges and would spend hours negotiating the 100-yard distance between the two greens, inventing shots with the different clubs. Arrowhead didn't have a short-game practice area, but I had my own. I hit long bunker shots, shots from deep grass, shots from hardpan and shots from every downhill, uphill, and sidehill lie you can imagine.

My dad had a teaching aid that he built himself—a spike with a magnet on the end of it. He'd put the magnet on the face of my club to show me what I was doing with the clubhead on short shots. I learned right away what turning the face down did to a chip—it makes it fly lower and run out more—and how to open the face of my 6-iron to hit a higher pitch shot.

Those basic lessons and hundreds of hours of experimentation were all I had when I went off to play competitively, first at USC and then out on tour. But as a young tour player, I was fortunate enough to have some friends and fellow competitors who were willing to show a young guy some other shots to play. Dale Douglass taught me a foolproof shot to use when you need to hit a short shot off a hardpan lie—which I'll show you in Chapter 6—and I reinvented my bunker technique after listening to an audio lesson from Julius Boros, who won three major championships with it. My dad actually found the recording and sent it to me, and I had to listen to it three times to get the most important piece of it—about focusing on the back edge of the club entering the sand—before I got it. We're going to talk more about that in the bunker chapter.

By the 1980s, I was winding down my PGA Tour career and getting ready for the Champions Tour. But I was still learning new things about the short game. My friend Tom Kite was the first player to incorporate a 60-degree wedge into his set. He used it to pitch-in on the 7th hole at Pebble Beach at the U.S. Open, and ended up winning the tournament by one. Tom convinced me to try out that club for myself. I had always been one of the top scramblers on tour, hitting everything with my 56-degree wedge. But adding another wedge gave me some other options, and it was a big reason why I was able to win nine tournaments in my first three years on the Champions Tour.

Through almost fifty years of tournament experience and more than forty-five years of working with players at every handicap level, I've come up with a simple approach to short-game shots that will take so much of the stress and fear out of that part of the game for you.

I've done the legwork, so to speak.

All you have to do is learn two simple shots.

Tell me if this sounds familiar. You've got a "standard" 20-yard shot from a good lie in front of the green. You take your 56-degree wedge, and nervously walk up to the ball. Your eyes lock onto the flag, and you make a couple of stiff, large practice swings. The shot that comes next is a sort of mid-height one, with a big backswing and a flip of the right hand to try to help the ball get into the air. You focused on the flag as your target and took a big backswing, but your subconscious brain knew the shot was going to go too far with that size swing, so it put on the brakes halfway down. So you hit a weak flip shot to the right, or you lifted your upper body and caught the ball with the leading edge and hit a grounder over the green.

Now, your short game might not be that bad. Maybe you're actually pretty good at hitting what I call an "in-between" shot, using both the left and right hands. I'll say right up front that there are many ways to chip and pitch the ball well. Hubert Green won a lot of tournaments and a lot of money bending way over and holding the shaft on the steel and flipping his hands at the ball. Phil Mickelson makes a big forward press and uses a lot of hand action on his short-game shots, while Raymond Floyd—who could be the best chipper ever—stood really close to the ball and didn't use any hand action at all. He's the only player I've ever seen who could have a per-fect, Augusta-caliber lie within 12 inches of the putting surface and choose to chip it. He was so good that he had just as much of a chance to make it that way as I would have had putting it.

But I'm here to tell you that you can make your short-game life so much easier if you give up hitting those in-between shots and start thinking of every short-game shot as either a high shot or a low shot. Once you've picked which shot best suits the situation—and we're going to talk about how to do just that in the next chapter—you can move on and concentrate on making the simple swing that produces the shot you picked.

For many of you, it's going to be hard to accept that the short game can be so straightforward. You're probably convinced that golf is a complicated game to learn, and that there are so many variables for each shot that it's impossible to consider them all. And many of you simply don't have any consistent technique or a decision-making process about what shot you want to play for a given situation.

Raymond Floyd (1) and Hubert Green (2) were two of the best chippers in the history of the game, and they each did it in a radically different way. Ray stood very close to the ball and very tall and used very little hand action, while Hubert crouched low, choked up, and flipped his hands at the ball. You can be great with a variety of techniques, but some are easier to master than others. Courtesy of *Golf Digest*

I'm going to help you with that.

In my dad's day, equipment wasn't nearly as good as it is now. The iron heads were tiny, and they all had sharp leading edges. So he perfected a basic, "safe" motion for a short-game shot, and then used a variety of clubs to change how high and far he hit each shot. He'd use anything from a 6-iron to a sand wedge on a variety of little pitches and bump-and-run shots around the green. For me, the problem with those clubs is that if you miss the ball slightly, you can't control the distance very well. One shot might check up when it hits, and another might go rolling away hot. But wedges (and hybrids, for that matter) are so well-designed today that they can almost hit the shot for you if you pick the right shot—low or high—for the lie and the situation. Now, if you grew up in Kansas or Scotland, you might have had to learn some specialty low shots with a flatter-faced club, but I'm confident in saying that you'll be able to have a very high-level short game using just your wedges and an occasional hybrid club (for the bump-and-run shots that we're going to talk about in Chapter 6).

Does this mean you're going to turn into some kind of short-game robot who goes out and hits mindless, cookie-cutter high and low shots? Of course not. What you're going to learn here is that the short game is broken up into low shots and high shots, each with their own basic technique, and that the finesse and art of the short game comes from using that basic technique to control the face of the club for the shot you want to hit.

I'll explain just how to do that in more detail in the next four chapters, but let me tell you a story about how I end all the short-game clinics I teach. As I'm wrapping up my talk, I'll take out my 60-degree wedge, hood the face and hit a low chip shot about 30 yards down the range. Then I'll hide the club behind me and ask the students in the class what club I used. They've just heard me talk about hitting a 56- or 60-degree wedge for most shots, so they almost always answer "sand wedge." I'll play along and ask, "Do you think the sand wedge really goes that low?" Then, most of the time, they change the answer to pitching wedge or 9-iron. Using the same club, I'll then hit a sky-high flop shot, and then show them the bottom of the wedge.

It's a 60-degree wedge.

The point is, you can and will be able to hit both kinds of shots with the same club, with more control over the clubface. It's the improvement in your technique that's going to give you that control—and it will give you something else that will transform your game: Confidence.

When I'm playing a shot from around the green, I'm trying to make every single one. And I believe that I will. The fact that I believe I can hole any short-game shot I have takes a tremendous amount of pressure off my long game. I'm not standing in the fairway thinking I've got to be perfect.

Once you develop these simple techniques for low and high shots and see that you have so much more control over the clubface than you believed, you will start to feel that same kind of confidence. Now, if you're a 20-handicapper, you're probably thinking it's crazy—or at least unreasonable—to believe that you should hole every short-game shot. Heck, you might be struggling just to make consistent contact right now. But I promise you, once you accept that there are two different shots to hit and see how straightforward they are, that confidence is going to grow.

You're going to start playing holes with a strategy and a purpose, and the belief that you can find an escape hatch if you need one. Golf is going to become much more like a chess match for you than a hit-it-and-hope exercise. At the minimum, you're going to feel like you can hit a positive shot from any location. If you're in the bunker, you'll be able to get out of the bunker. If you're in deep grass, you'll be able to get back into position. You're going to be able to finish holes and finish rounds, instead of letting them finish you.

After all, who doesn't want to be the player nobody wants to face in match play? Think about who that is at your club or course. It isn't the player who can bomb it off the tee.

It's the one who can make a score.

TWO

Increasing Your
Short-game Awareness

I'm not revealing any big secrets when I say that golf is a target-oriented game. When you're standing on the tee and looking out over the hole in front of you, everything you see is geared toward sending the ball to a target—either a part of the fairway or, eventually, the flag on the green.

That simplicity is one of the beauties of the game, but it also causes players a lot of trouble when it comes to the short game. They get so conscious of the flag that they lose track of the important decisions that go into hitting effective scoring shots.

In this chapter, I want to take you through my decision-making and visualization process for shots I hit around the green. I'm going to help you pick what shot to hit—high or low—and show you how to see that shot before you hit it. And seeing it ahead of time is an extremely important part of the deal—not something to discount as soft or unimportant. I've done it on every short-game shot I've hit in tournament play over the last forty-five years. It's just as important—if not more important—than the actual mechanics.

Picking the right shot starts with accurately assessing your situation and understanding what options your situation offers. And nothing is more important than being able to accurately diagnose your lie. The lie dictates what is possible. Once you have the list of what's possible, then you can pick what shot will work best.

When I walk up the fairway to the green area and get to my ball, the first thing I do is crouch down and take a good look at my lie. You obviously can have every lie under the sun, from perfect fairway to deep grass to bare, dry hardpan. The most important factor in determining how you see the potential shots around you is whether or not you can cleanly get the club on the back of the ball.

When a ball sits on a perfect fairway lie, or even in light rough, the entire back of the ball is exposed, and you can make clean contact with your club. When you can make that clean contact with the ball before the club hits the ground, you have the most control—and therefore the most choices. When I can make clean contact with the back of the ball, I'm most often going to hit a low shot. The exceptions would be if I need to carry a ball over a tier or other problem area between me and the hole. In tournament situations, a good 80 to 85 percent of all shots I hit around the green are low shots, and most of those are with one of the three wedges in my bag: the 48-, 54-, or 60-degree, depending on how much carry I need.

If the ball is nestled in deeper grass, or in a divot or other imperfect lie (or if I need to hit a high shot to carry some kind of trouble or steep slope between me and the target), it's time to play a high shot with a bunker-type motion. On a high shot, you use the bounce on the bottom of the club to strike the ground first. The club skims through the grass and dirt and shoots the ball up in the air. How close you hit to the ball determines how much spin you put on the shot. We'll talk more about that in Chapter 3, when I introduce you to the high shot.

Average players make two big mistakes when it comes to deciphering lies. The first is that they attempt to play most shots from around the green with the same in-between technique. The second is underestimating the influence that lie has on a shot. The problem is that most 20-handicappers aren't very consistent in their short game, so when they hit a bad chip, they aren't really clear if it was because of a bad swing, or a poor shot selection given the lie and situation. Even if you didn't change your technique, your short game would improve if you improved your understanding of how the club and ball respond from different lies. If you can't hit the back of the ball cleanly, making a small swing or digging the leading edge of the club into the ground doesn't give you much of a chance to get a good result.

You might think this is a lot of time to devote to the smallest details of reading lies, but I can tell you from painful experience that it's important to get it right. One of the major mistakes in my career came at the 1976 Masters. I was in contention on Sunday, and on the par-5 15th I had to lay up short of the creek. I had 75 yards over the water for my third shot. I looked at my lie, and all I could see was perfect Augusta green. But as I took the club back, I saw that the ball was actually sitting on a perfectly groomed bit of green sand. The club goes around and fills divots with green sand and seed so that the fairway looks perfect on television. And they do such a good job that it's hard to tell the difference between the sand and the grass. I figured the difference out too late. I was into my downswing, prepared for a certain kind of impact and the way the club would move through the grass. All of a sudden, I wasn't seeing the same shot I had pictured. I dumped it into the lake and made seven.

The position of the pin is the second most important factor to consider after your lie—but only in the sense that it leads you to pick a high shot or a low one. See if you can recognize yourself in this example: The average player walks up to his or her ball and is almost 100 percent focused on the flag. There might be a brief thought about the lie, and if the ball is on fairway grass or in the rough. In fact, many players would secretly prefer to hit a short-game shot from rough because they feel like they can scoop under the ball more easily and get it airborne.

Then, after a second look at the lie, the player tries a standard in-between pitch shot with the hole as the target. Even if he or she hits it exactly as he wanted, the ball hits near the flag and rolls out too far.

In my routine, the flag is certainly the ultimate target, but it isn't my main focus. After I've decided to hit a low shot, I visualize the entire shot, as though I'm seeing a video replay of it after I've hit it. I see where the ball lands, how it bounces, how much it checks or rolls out, and where it eventually ends up—in the cup. That visualization process changes my focus from the flag to the spot on which I want the ball to initially land.

I'll watch amateur players chip and pitch early in one of my clinics, and even if they understand this concept they'll almost always be aimed with their feet and body cheating in the direction of the flag. For example, if you have a 50-foot chip with a lot of green between you and the flag, but a good 10 feet of right-to-left break, and you play a low, running chip, you obviously need to aim for a spot to the right of a straight line between you and the hole. But even when players know this, they still get drawn toward aiming at the flag—almost as though it was a magnet. The concept is the same for a high shot, but with a slightly different technique. On a high shot, I'm visualizing the trajectory the ball will take out of the grass, and where it will land on the green. Then I'm picturing how much the ball will trickle out after it lands.

After the quality of your lie, the landing point for your shot is the most important single piece of information you need to figure out on a short-game shot. You're trying to pick the spot that gives you the cleanest, simplest path toward the target—or that leaves you with the easiest putt possible. On 95 percent of all shots, that means landing the ball on a relatively flat part of the green. On rare occasions, you may need to land the ball on the face of a slope and bounce it up, or land the ball in fairway or fringe grass, but the over-whelming number of "basic" shots you're going to play will involve picking a landing area on the green.

As we talked about with your lie, the shot you end up playing will be heavily influenced by where you decide the ball needs to land for the best chance to get close. Take a "basic" shot from 10 yards off the green, with 30 feet of green between the edge of the fringe and the cup. The green itself is relatively flat, with some slight right-to-left break around the hole. I'm going to play a shot that flies over the fairway grass and fringe and lands five feet on the green and runs out the rest of the way like a putt. I will visualize the extremely specific shot path and landing point, and how the ball will roll out during its time on the ground.

If I have a shot of the same distance with the same amount of green to work with, but the flag is up on a high tier, my landing spot and shot choice will probably be different. Say the tier starts 10 feet onto the green, and the flag is up on the tier with 10 feet of flat green in front and 10 feet behind. I would then choose a shot that flies over the fairway and fringe grass and carries the front slope of the tier, landing on top in the flat area. My landing point would be closer to the hole, giving myself some margin for error, since a miss long—and still on the flat part of the tier—is far better than missing short and watching the ball roll back down the tier.

As I said before, a vast majority of the shots that I hit in tournament play are low shots. Unless you play a lot at a course with some extremely undu-lating greens, you're probably going to end up playing at least 80 percent of your short-game shots with the low technique we're going to talk about in the next chapter. With a little bit of experience, you're going to be able to make a decent assessment of your lie and landing point and know if a basic low shot is going to work, or if you're going to need loft to get the ball out of the grass or carry something that's between you and the hole.

But just like any other skill, seeing shot options and executing them takes time and practice. The bottom line is that you need to hit a lot of shots and see for yourself how the ball reacts off the face of your club, and how it rolls out when you use the two techniques we're going to talk about. One of the most effective ways you can spend your time at the range, bar none, is at the short-game area. You might hit twelve or thirteen drivers in a round, but you'll hit fifty or more shots from 30 yards and in. You tell me: Which kinds of shots make the most sense to practice more?

I love watching Phil Mickelson go through his short-game practice routine. He'll take four balls and drop them in a spot next to the practice green, pick a specific shot to one of the holes and hit it, then pick a different shot to a different hole, and so on. He'll hit four different shots to four different holes, walk a circuit and pick up the balls and do it again. He's painting a picture of different shots in his head, and working on his feel for each of them.

Start your practice routine by picking just one shot, a low one, with your lob wedge. Choose a hole to play to, but pick as your first target the spot on the green where you think the ball needs to land so that it ends up by that hole. Stick a tee or a Stockton Golf Ring in the green on that spot, and then hit three or four practice shots. Then pick a different hole and do the same exercise, hitting three or four high shots to the tee you picked as the right landing spot. At the beginning, most players either don't come close to landing the ball near the tee, or the shots that do land near the tee don't end up anywhere near the hole.

If that's you, don't get discouraged. You're getting a lot of great information about your short game, and feedback about what you need to practice. If you have trouble consistently hitting the area around the tee, you need to pay close attention to the next chapter and improve your low-shot technique. If you can consistently land the ball near the tee, but the shot isn't ending up near the hole, you aren't picking the right landing area. You're not seeing the best shot for the situation.

What is the "best" shot? It's one that goes in the hole, of course, but there's more to it than that. I'm certainly trying to make every shot I hit, and I want you to have that belief for yourself. But you do need to be influenced and informed by the situation at hand. Visualizing the path of your shot also includes seeing where it will come to rest if it doesn't go in the hole. If you have a shot to a pin with a dramatic drop-off in front or behind, you need to weigh those risks when you plan your shot. If that drop-off is behind the hole, any shot you play probably shouldn't be too far past the hole if you miss. You're going to be better off just short, if anything. The opposite is true if the tier is in front of the flag.

You'll see this strategic concept happen all the time in tournament golf. Tour players always look for the area around the flag with the most relatively flat space, and they favor that space as a buffer area for a potential miss. At Augusta National, for example, players would almost always prefer a 10- or 15-foot putt with relatively little break than a three-footer with a sharp curve. That fact dictates very strongly where some short-game shots need to go. These players have the greatest skill in the world, and they are very willing to play conservative shots around the green when necessary. That should tell you that you need to consider the same strategy when you're presented with a difficult pin with danger spots on one side or another.

The only way to get a sense for the best place to leave a shot is to walk up to the hole before you play and make an assessment. On any shot from 30 yards and in, I'll make a quick trip up to the green with my eyes on the ground, looking for any tiers or slopes that would be bad places to land my chip or pitch. I'll then walk up to the hole and look for changes in slope that might be hard to see from farther away. In *Unconscious Putting* (and in Chapter 10 of this book, if you need a refresher), I described how crucial it is to break each putt into thirds, with the final third of the putt being the most important because a ball that is slowing down is more influenced by break. That same philosophy needs to guide the way you look at your short-game shots from off the green. Looking at the last third of your short-game shots— whether they're low ones running out like a putt or lofted ones that hit and roll out just a few feet—will get you thinking about how the ball will take any break around the hole. You will hole out a lot more chips and pitches—and leave the rest of them closer—when you start looking at the end of these shots, just like you would a putt.

I don't usually look at putts from behind the hole, but it can be useful to check out a chip shot from back there because you can get an overall sense of the green's topography from the hole to where your ball is. You're also more likely to want to leave a short-game shot a few feet or more past the hole, while I'm always trying to hit a putt no more than 16 inches beyond the cup.

So much of golf is played in carts now, and I think that's a shame, for a lot of reasons. You don't get as much exercise that way, and you're also robbed of a lot of the intuitive sense of how a hole is designed. When you walk up to the green from the fairway, you can feel the changes in slope and topography with your feet and see it with your eyes. When you speed up to the side of the hole in a cart and go back to your ball, you have to make a special effort to see the entire green complex in that same way.

The only good thing is that speeding up in that cart can give you a little extra time to see your shot. Even if you're walking and carrying your bag—or playing with a caddie—I'm not an advocate of holding up play by taking an exorbitant amount of time reviewing every angle between your ball and the hole. My routine is the same speed if I'm playing a round for fun as it is during a tournament. I'll walk up to the green with my wedge in my hand to check out my shot while my playing partners are heading to their balls. I might stop briefly to study the area around the flag, but I'm headed back to my ball within 10 or 20 seconds. By the time I get back to my ball, I already know what shot I want to play. If I need to change to a different club—which is rare—I'll do that, then immediately go into my pre-shot routine and play the shot I see in my mind.

My last piece of advice about shot selection has to do with confidence and conviction. If you go through your process and pick a shot for the given situation, it's more important to believe you're hitting the right shot—and to look forward to hitting it—than it is for the actual shot selection to be the right one. If it feels like a situation in which you want to hit a high shot, hit one. Doubt and negativity are worse for your game than a less-than-perfect strategic decision.

THREE

Low Shots

It's amazing what loft can do to a player.

We always start our Stockton Golf clinics with putting, and even the players with the biggest problems in that department can usually roll the ball with some idea of where it is going. And after thirty minutes of basic instruction—essentially, the contents of Chapter 10—a vast majority of players are pretty comfortable on the putting green.

But when you take a lot of players just a few steps off the green—far enough away that it starts to become clear that they need to hit some kind of chip—strange things start to happen.

I see it even in players who are otherwise good players. They can hit a 250-yard tee shot and knock an iron up by the green, but they just disintegrate when they have a chip shot.

In reality, a straightforward low shot from a good lie to a pin in an accessible location shouldn't be much more complicated than a putt from the same distance on the green.

I know I just caused a whole lot of you to shake your head and think to yourself, "Easy for you to say." But it's true. With a basic understanding of how to position yourself and think about the shot, a low chip can become your go-to option for a majority of the situations you face around the green.

When you watch a guy who is an absolute artist at chipping, like Raymond Floyd, set up to that shot, he's thinking about holing every single one. And he's genuinely surprised when the ball doesn't go in. I know I'm thinking the same thing when I play my average low shot. I'm not hoping to just get it up there somewhere within 10 feet, or just get it on the green.

Sure, you're thinking, tour players have different expectations because they have more talent. We do, but talent isn't what holds the average player back. With some minor technical improvements and a clearer understanding of what you're trying to do with the shot, there's no reason why, after a little practice, you can't be almost as proficient at low shots as anybody. And, more importantly, why you can't have the aggressive "I'm going to make this" attitude that so many good players have.

You tell me: Are your results going to be better when you're standing over a chip shot just hoping to get it on the green without chunking it or skulling it, or will they be better if you're thinking about nothing but the path the ball is going to take into the hole?

Let's start by talking about why many players struggle to hit what is really a pretty simple shot.

In putting, you can (within reason) get away with a variety of different stances and setups and still roll the ball effectively. That's because you're putting the flat face of the putter onto the back of the ball, above the level of the ground. You aren't worried about the lie, and you're not worried about having to get the ball into the air.

With a low chip shot, you've got some other variables to contend with, obviously. But the way players respond to those variables often makes the shot way harder to hit consistently. Setup problems are far and away the biggest obstacle separating a bad chipper from a good one.

Now, if you watched Hubert Green hit chip shots, you'd see a guy who did just about the opposite of everything I'm about to describe. And he, along with Raymond Floyd, was hands down one of the two best chippers I've ever seen. Hubert choked way down on the club, to the point where his hands were holding onto the steel, and he crouched down and flipped his hands at the ball.

But the truth is, he hit so many great shots because he had a gifted set of hands. The same is true for Raymond Floyd—even though his setup is closer to what I'd call ideal. In fact, Raymond's technique just confirmed for me what I learned from guys like Dale Douglass when I first came out on tour: innate touch is great, obviously, but the key to being a consistent chipper is the ability to make consistent contact with the ball. If the club hits the ball the same way every time, you're going to have a good idea where it's going.

A vast majority of amateur players address a chip shot—or any short-game shot, really—with the idea that they're going to have to lift the ball into the air. They get into the mind-set that they're going to have to have a lot of control over the clubhead, so they grip the handle tightly, bend over more, and then scoop at the ball at the bottom of the swing. In the meantime, they lift up out of the posture they started from.

Unless you have a genius kind of touch like Hubert Green, it's really hard to hit a ball forward with any kind of consistency or feel when you're scooping and coming up on it like that.

Your goals on a low shot are pretty simple, then. You want to set up taller to the ball and stay tall through the shot, and you want to make consistent contact with the ball first, before the club hits the ground.

To preset your body for these two goals, you're going to stand to the ball in a way that will probably feel a little strange at first. Move two or three inches closer to the ball than you'd stand for a putt—about six or eight

In a good low-shot setup, the feet are shoulder-width apart and turned toward the target, and the weight is mostly on the lead foot (1). Players run into problems when the feet get very narrow (2), which prevents the weight from ever getting to the lead leg, or when they widen the stance and bend over too far (3). You'll tend to lift up and scoop the ball from this position.

inches away from it, if you drew a line in front of your toes and measured the distance from that line to the ball—and set your feet slightly closer together than they would be on a putt—about a foot apart. Distribute your weight so that most of it is on your lead leg—which will keep the bottom of your swing in front of the ball. I've heard some teachers say it's important to have a narrow stance for chipping, but I think that makes it very hard to keep that weight on the lead leg. When your stance is that narrow, the tendency is to hang back on the back foot, drop the shoulders through impact and try to lift the ball. I don't like any of those things.

One thing you'll notice when you set up closer to the ball is that the club will naturally want to start at a more upright angle. If you were standing on pavement, you'd be able to clearly see the clubhead resting on its toe and the rest of the sole of the club up off the ground. That's not a mistake. You're exposing the widest part of the clubface to the ball for solid contact, but you're reducing the area of the sole that could get snagged in the grass. If you catch the shot slightly toward the toe or heel, you'll still get a decent result.

From that taller position (on a level lie), you're going to grip the club to its full length and not choke down on it at all. I use the same grip on my low shots as I do for a full swing—a standard overlapping grip. If you want to use the same grip as you do for putting, that's fine. I'm in favor of whatever grip gives you the best feel. I do believe the grip needs to be neutral, though. If you let the grip drift too strong, so that the V's created by your thumbs and the sides of your hands turn toward your right shoulder vs. your right collarbone, you'll tend to turn the clubhead over through impact. That reduces the loft on the face, and exposes more of the leading edge of the club to the ground, where it can snag. Paul Runyan always taught an extreme short-game grip that had the right and left hands turned way over to the opposite sides of the handle. I don't teach that grip, but if you're going to get away from one that's neutral, at least go in Paul's direction and have the hands opposing each other equally.

The last adjustment you need to make to your stance is to simply turn both of your feet toward the target. You can set up with your feet square and perpendicular to the target line, keep your heels in place and shift your toes about 45 degrees toward the target. What this does is make it much easier for your weight to stay forward at address and your body to release toward

On a low shot, ball position is back of center, in line with the right big toe. The hands are centered, which puts the grip slightly ahead of the ball at address. From this position, it's easy to hit the ball first and then the ground.

the target through the swing. We're trying to do everything we can to avoid having weight hanging back on the back foot.

Once you've spent the time to get your setup right, don't waste all of that preparation by getting careless with your ball position. On a standard low shot, I play the ball off the big toe of my right foot—and remember, my right foot is turned toward the target. That puts the ball back in my stance, about three inches behind center. That position will slightly adjust back and forward depending on the shot I want to hit—back for lower and forward for higher. My hands stay centered in front of my body, so the back ball position angles the shaft slightly toward the target. When you set up this way, you're putting the club in position to swing down and hit the ball on the downswing—before it reaches the bottom of its arc, and before it hits the ground.

If you let your ball position drift too far toward the middle, you run the risk of hitting the ground before the ball unless you make some other change in your swing. This change is often a scoop move with the hands to avoid hitting the clubhead into the ground—and to lift the ball. And, as we've been talking about, that move can be a short-game killer. When we talk about high shots in the next chapter, you'll see a major difference in ball position when the goal is to release the clubhead, not move the left hand down the target line as you would for a low shot like this.

With the club set so that the shaft is angled slightly toward the target, you've effectively reduced the loft on the face of the club. That's OK, because your 56- or 60-degree wedge still has plenty of built-in loft to get the ball up in the air without you doing anything extra with your hands to help it.

When I was learning the short game from my dad back at Arrowhead Country Club in San Bernardino, he would stick a magnet with a spike attached to it onto the face of my wedge and have me set up to different short shots. Just by looking down at how the spike extended from the face, I was able to train my eye to see the effect that even small adjustments in the clubface had on loft. If you adjust the handle of the club so that it's vertical—as we will on high shots in the next chapter—it adds a significant amount of loft to the shot. And when you open the face of the club, it produces even more loft, and some left-to-right side-spin. With the spike, it's easy to see why you need to adjust your aiming point to the left when you play shots with an open clubface. You can buy the magnetized spikes now as a training aid, and they also work great for the long game. You can instantly see how your setup

Subtle changes in how the club is set at address can dramatically change the height and direction of the shot. The spike simulates the trajectory of the shot, which ranges from medium with the club soled flat (1), to high with the shaft moved back for a lob shot (2), and to super high when the clubface is opened, as it would be for some bunker shots (3).

impacts trajectory, and whether or not your shot is going to clear an obstacle in front of you.

Now that you're in position to hit the shot, how should it actually feel to do it? Like a gentle underhanded toss. If I gave you a golf ball and asked you to make a low toss from off the green and get the ball rolling toward the hole, you'd gently move your arm back and load your wrist, then pivot toward the target with your lower body as you unloaded your wrist and let the ball go from your fingertips. You wouldn't freeze your entire lower body and stiffly toss the ball with just your arm, which would cause your upper body to lift up.

The motion and feel of a low shot is the same as you'd get if you tossed a ball underhanded and low along the green. The right leg releases slightly toward the target and the chest stays level.

You're trying to replicate the simplicity and feel of that underhand toss while actually holding on to a golf club. The only swing thought I ever use on a low shot—once I've visualized the shot itself and my landing target—is that I'm going to start the swing with the back of my left hand, pushing the club straight away from the target. This is going to feel strange to you if you're used to trying to make the clubhead move more and faster on your short shots, because these motions are dominated by the right hand.

Instead, I want you to try to initiate the swing with that push-away move. The club will stay low to

The backswing motion is dominated by the feeling of pushing the clubhead back with the back of the left hand. The right hand moves in response to the left, and the clubhead loads slightly but stays low (1). Notice how the back of the left wrist stays straight and in line with the arm (2). There's no hit in this stroke.

the ground, and the right wrist will give a little so that the clubhead loads, but you're not consciously cocking your wrists and doing anything to increase the speed of the clubhead. I don't even refer to the second part of the shot as a "downswing," because I don't want to encourage any kind of hit move with the right hand as the clubhead heads down to the ball. Just as when I'm putting, I'm just moving the back of my left hand toward the target. The club is an extension of my arms, and the ball just gets in the way as I sweep through.

Because you've set up with your weight on your front foot and your feet shoulder-width apart and angled toward the hole, you've made it easier for your legs to work naturally through the shot. Your right heel should release so that your knee moves toward the hole. If your stance is too narrow and you don't get off your back foot, your knee will tend to move straight out, away from you, and you'll hang back or lift up through impact. This will often result in a fat shot. Remember, the goal is to set your posture tall at address and keep it that way through the shot. That applies to both lifting up through impact and dipping down to try to hit the ball.

By allowing your lower body to move in a fluid, natural way, your upper body can stay fairly quiet. I feel like my chest stays tall and parallel to the target

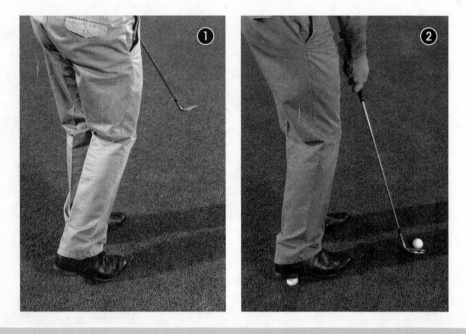

The lower body definitely has a role in the low shot. Start with your weight on your lead leg and let the right heel release as you make a small turn through the shot (1). One way to accentuate this feel is to hit some shots with a ball under your right heel (2).

line while my arms remain close to my body through the entire swing. I'm not making a big shoulder turn, as I would for a full pitch or a regular iron shot. After all, the goal here is not to produce power, but to make precise contact.

After I make contact with the ball, my clubhead stays low to the ground—I can easily just drop it and tap the grass. It never gets more than a foot above the ground after impact. I've turned through with my upper body toward the target, but it's not a conscious turn. It's more of a natural reaction to the lower body pivoting and the arms moving. We're talking about a very easygoing, quiet shot here, with the same pace and tempo on the backswing as in the forward swing.

Almost without exception, bad chippers either hurt themselves with an impossible setup, or they're the ones who make a fast backswing and go fast to the ball with a lot of right-hand action. They end up scooping at it, and they finish with the club hoisted up and around to the left. They've moved the clubhead in a huge arc around their body for a shot that needs to go maybe 20 yards. All that extra size and speed can only get you in trouble.

On the backswing, the lower body pivots slightly, while the upper body stays pretty quiet (1). As the legs flow toward the target, the right knee releases down toward the ball (2)—there's no hit move in the hands. Your thought after impact is to move the back of the left hand toward the hole and keep the clubhead low (3).

When it comes to changing the distance and height of the shot you want to hit, I don't want you to think about making a faster swing. The swing just gets a little longer, and you adjust the trajectory either by slightly adjusting your shaft angle forward or backward, or by using a different club.

On every low shot, I pick the exact spot on the green I want the ball to land, and then I visualize the exact shot that will produce that flight to that spot with the right amount of roll-out afterward. As we talked about in the last chapter, you're picking that spot by taking into consideration what trouble you have to carry and what the ball is going to do once it hits the ground and starts rolling like a putt. For that part of the shot, you're reading the green exactly the way you would for a putt.

Pick your landing point on the green and make that the focus when you set your aim. Make it as specific as possible.

Once you've hit some low shots with this technique and you start to make consistent contact, you'll get a sense for how high and far the ball will go with a "standard" 56- or 60-degree swing. For me, I'm not usually hitting a low shot from more than 30 or 35 yards in total distance, or from more than 10 paces off the green. Once I get to that total distance, I'm going to hit a pitch shot that has some backspin on it, which gives me a lot of precision in terms of where I can land the ball and stop it. But practically speaking, there's no reason why you couldn't hit a longer low shot that landed on close-cut fringe grass and rolled back to the target, especially if it's a shot you like better than an off-distance short pitch. That's a common shot in places like Scotland or the Southwest U.S., where the ground is really firm and the wind blows. The shot Charl Schwartzel hit on the first hole at Augusta National on the Sunday of the tournament was one of the best short-game shots of 2011—a long, low-running pitch that landed in front of the green and rolled all the way across it and into the hole. He might be the only player in the world who would have tried that shot at that time, and I think it was the key shot to his victory.

Improving your ability to see the right shot for the situation, pick the right landing spot, and then hit it is definitely the art of this part of the game. What I want you to understand is that the mechanical skill to produce that kind of art isn't hard to develop to at least a playable level. Missing your landing spot by a foot or two is far less damaging to the outcome than potentially chunking it or blading it with an awkward, in-between technique. At our clinics, players routinely come in with a 20- or 25-handicapper's skill level at low shots and leave with a 10-handicapper's ability after just a couple of hours of work.

It's not brain surgery.

The best part is that you don't have to be close to perfect. Follow these setup guidelines and you can catch shots far less than perfectly and still end up OK. Your misses will be five or six feet from the hole instead of being in tap-in range.

I bet you could live with that.

FOUR

High Shots

It'd be nice if every short-game shot came with a perfect lie and a flat path to the hole the width of a driveway. But that's obviously not how it goes.

When you can't get the club onto the back of the ball cleanly, or you need to carry some obstacle or uneven piece of terrain between the ball and the hole, you need to hit a shot that goes up in the air.

The simplest way to do that is to think about it as a completely different shot than the one you learned in the last chapter. It is not a modified version of the low shot. The simplest way to think about the relationship between the two is to consider the low shot as a left-hand-dominated one—like a putt—and the high shot as a right-handed-dominated shot.

In the low shot, the left hand starts the action, and the swing thought through the forward swing is related to moving the back of the left hand toward the hole. The right hand doesn't do much more than hold on and respond to what is happening—or not happening—with the left.

On a high shot, we're going to make some slight modifications to the setup, and change the relationship between the two hands. To hit the ball high, you need to have loft on the clubface and to generate some more speed on the clubhead. To do that, the left hand plays a passive role, and the right hand controls what is happening in the shot.

Before you get worried that I'm going to give some complicated movement to learn, let me tell you that this shot is only slightly more involved than the low one. If you can keep a few major principles in mind as you practice it, you're going to swing the club with the bottom of its arc in a consistent place almost every time. Once you can do that—and it's never taken a student more than an hour or two to learn it at one of our clinics—you'll be equipped to hit almost any shot that you might face.

Then, all you have to do is work on seeing the shot you want to hit.

Let's start with the setup.

Many players get into a situation where they need to hit a shot with some loft and they make a series of extreme changes to their stance with the idea that an extremely open stance or clubface or a steep shoulder tilt is going to solve the entire problem. They choke up on the club, grab the handle very tightly, bend way over and spread way out, lower the right shoulder, and physically try to lift the ball into the air. They get into those positions because they *think* they have more control over a small motion with the club. It seems to make intuitive sense that you could have precise control over a 10- or 20-yard shot by controlling the handle of the club and trying to force it into the right positions. They take the club back very short, and then explode into the ball by driving the handle of the club hard to the left—which produces drive on the shot instead of lift. The result? A line drive across the green, or a chunk of sod ripped out of the ground just off the green.

It doesn't need to be so hard.

Instead of setting up in a way that makes sense in your head—but not on the shot itself—let's try setting up in a way that makes sense in relation to how the body actually moves for a fluid, effective high shot. Just like with the low shot, I want my weight starting mostly on my front foot, and my feet turned toward the target so that I'm set up to keep the weight there throughout the shot. I'm relatively close to the ball and feel as though I'm as tall as I can be—with my grip and the end of the handle and my shoulders pulled slightly back. Both of my knees are flexed gently, and I'm keeping the feeling of looseness in my arms and hands. When you start with a wide stance and your feet aimed straight at your target line, you've preset yourself to hang back through impact, even if you start out with your weight favoring your lead leg. This shot is all about feel—not power—and your goal is to keep that touch and feel throughout your body instead of strangling it.

You have some grip options on the low shot depending on whether or not you want to copy the feel of a putter in your hands. But on a high shot, a reverse overlap putting grip is not going to work because you need your right hand to be more active. I like to use the same grip on this shot that I use for a full iron shot—a standard overlapping grip, taking care not to let

Some common setup problems include aiming the feet—especially the right foot—too square to the target line and pushing the hands ahead stiffly (1), and setting up too crouched over in a stance that's too wide (2).

the right hand drift too far onto the top of the club in a weak position. If the right hand gets too weak, you're going to have trouble swinging through impact with the face of the club open. The tendency will be to turn the club-head over and reduce the loft on the face—the opposite of what we're trying to accomplish.

When I set my grip on the handle, the outside edge of my left pinkie finger is just below the edge of the butt of the grip. I basically have my hands as far up on the end of the handle as they can go. This does two things. First, by making the club itself longer, you don't need to swing as hard to make the ball go a given distance. Second, when you grip the end of the handle, you can feel the weight in the clubhead much more easily. For me, it almost feels as though the clubhead wants to sling down through the ball without too much of a throwing effort from my right hand. When you choke up on the grip and can't feel that head, you have to be more aggressive with your hand action, which puts you at risk for shifting the handle toward the target instead of letting the right wrist unhinge and the left hand stop.

The high-shot grip is the same as the one you would use for a full iron shot, with the Vs of the thumbs pointing at the right collar on your shirt (1). The thumb and forefinger of the right hand (2) start the swing by pulling the clubhead back. There is about a half inch of handle exposed at the end of the grip (3).

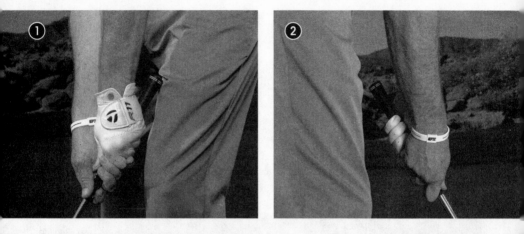

When you choke down on the handle, you reduce the length of the club and require a lot more swing speed to produce the same-size shot. It also prevents you from standing tall, and the head tends to lift.

With your weight forward and your feet shoulder-width apart and angled slightly toward the target, you want to position the ball so that your clubhead is vertical or slightly forward pressed—just inside the logo on the left breast of your shirt. With your weight forward and the shaft angled this way, you're set up to make a steeper, more up-and-down swing, which produces more height and backspin.

On the low shot, the backswing feel is that of a push away from the ball with the back of the left hand—much like the feeling of just getting the putter moving along the ground and the ball getting in the way. On the high shot, my feel is that I'm taking the club away with the thumb and index finger of my right hand, and picking the club up on a steep, vertical plane. It feels like I'm getting ready to toss a dart underhanded. I'm picking the clubhead up with those two fingers, letting the weight of the clubhead pull my right wrist into a full hinge at the top of the backswing, and then swinging the clubhead through while keeping the face open the entire way.

To keep that face open and working under the ball, you need to swing the clubhead down through impact and keep the right hand moving toward the target while the left hand stops roughly in the same position it was in at address. It's important to hit practice shots with this idea in mind, because some players run into two common problems. They either move both hands

You can see from the difference between the address (1) and top of the backswing photographs (2) that the weight has stayed on the front leg and the backswing is almost 80 percent of a full one. The right hand unloads the clubhead and the loft on the face pitches the ball straight up in the air (3). Notice how all of the lower-body momentum is moving toward the target.

Players who struggle with lofted shots start out from a much wider, more slouched address position (1) and make a short, arms-only backswing (2). With the feet aimed straight at the target line, the tendency is to hang back through the shot and try to lift the ball instead of letting the loft of the clubhead produce the height (3).

from the top of the backswing down and hard toward the hole, which shifts the grip toward the target and keeps the face and leading edge aimed toward the ground. At best, this produces a shot with no height, and at worst it produces a fat or skulled shot. The other common problem is that they pull the clubhead inside on a too-flat plane on the backswing, and then turn the clubhead over in the wrong direction and hood the face on the way through impact. That also produces some ugly misses.

Essentially, the high shot should feel like a 70 to 80 percent version of your full swing, with the same calm tempo on the backswing and forward swing and the right hand working palm-up through impact. It will feel like your right hand is passing under your left after impact and slinging the clubhead on its vertical plane straight at the target, with you just riding out the swing to a full finish. Again, this is a short shot that doesn't require much power, so you aren't going to be making a huge turn back or through the shot. But at the finish, your shoulders and hips will get pulled around

On a high shot, the club works on a very vertical plane, and it should feel like your right wrist is hinging the club up over the crown of your head, not around behind your neck (1). On the downswing, the right wrist unhinges and passes the left hand, which has stopped basically where it was at address (2).

naturally and will be facing the target, and the clubhead should finish high and in front of you—not pulled around so that the grip is near your left hip.

The setup basics we talked about make it very easy to make contact with the ground at virtually the same spot every time. Your next job is to determine where you want that spot to be in relation to the ball.

To me, this is where the high shot starts to get pretty cool, because on most shots you don't have to be extremely precise about where you hit behind the ball. Sure, if you make contact right on the back of the ball—or hit the club into the ground six inches behind it—you're going to get some bad results.

But if you let your right hand and clubhead work down through impact pointing up, you can hit anywhere from three inches to an inch behind the ball and the wedge will do the work of popping the ball out of the grass, just like a bunker shot.

You're probably asking yourself what happens when you have a super-firm lie. Unless you're hitting the shot from concrete, even firm turf won't keep you from being able to execute this shot, as long as you keep the bounce on the sole of the club exposed to the ground throughout the impact area. I'm not going to mislead you and say that hitting a shot like this from tight fairway grass to clear a water hazard is an easy shot, but you do have some room for error. Just keep the risks in mind when you're picking the shot. There's not much risk from lusher grass, but if you're hitting from tight grass or a bad lie, the shot will fly shorter than you anticipate if you hit a little too far behind the ball. You want to make sure that's the difference between having a 20-footer or 5-footer, not the difference between carrying the hazard itself and hitting it close. A long putt for par or birdie is always better than the risk of putting yourself in even worse position with a substandard high shot.

Tournament golf has a way of making a lot of those choices for you. Most times, you're going to want to pick the risk-free shot. But coming down the stretch, you may not have that choice. When I hit that high shot from hardpan on the 13th hole at the 1970 PGA, there wasn't anywhere else but that five-foot spot on the top of the ridge where I could have landed my ball. I knocked it to a foot, and it might have been the best short-game shot I've ever hit in any tournament, given the circumstances. I ended up winning by two shots—ones I would have given back (plus more, probably) if my ball had carried a foot or two longer and rolled off that ledge.

After you've perfected the setup and swing basics, your job is going to be to visualize the specific height and landing point for your shot, and to make slight setup and swing adjustments to produce that shot shape.

You can increase the height on the shot you're about to hit with a few subtle adjustments. Opening the face obviously produces more effective loft on the club, but the more dramatically you open it, the more you risk hitting the shot off the hosel. You can get the same loft effect by opening the face slightly and also shifting the shaft so that it has no forward press at address. The more vertical the shaft is, the more effective loft you have on the face. You can certainly use a club with extreme loft built in, like the 64-degree wedge Phil Mickelson sometimes carries. We'll talk in more detail about equipment in a later chapter, but I'll say here that I don't think the risks that come with a 64-degree club are worth the extra height you could produce with a 60-degree wedge, especially for the amateur player. If you have decent technique, you can hit virtually any shot you need with a 58- or 60-degree club. The one or two times a month you face something that might be better played with a 64-degree isn't worth losing the flexibility of the lower-lofted club for so many other shots around the green.

As far as distance control on a high shot goes, there's no magic formula

The angle of the shaft at address has an impact on the height of the shot you produce. When the shaft is pressed slightly forward (1), it reduces the effective loft of the club. By shifting the shaft back to a neutral, vertical position (2) and opening the face slightly, you can hit a much higher shot.

that will tell you how hard to swing for a certain shot. I think you'll find that the size of your swing is pretty consistent for most 10- to 20-yard high shots, with the difference in carry distance and height coming from the speed at which you unload the clubhead with your right hand through impact.

I wish I could tell you that there's a shorter road to developing feel for distance, but it really comes from hitting a variety of shots and making the connection between the swing, the quality and location of contact, and the distance the ball goes. There are dozens of variables that come into play, from the kind of grass you're playing from to the speed of the green you're playing to. In that regard, any short-game shot is very much like putting, in that the art comes from the quality of judgment more than the technical execution of the stroke.

I will say that building some competence and confidence in the high shot will bail you out of some iffy visualization and decision-making and give you a very nice cushion. You can pick the wrong landing spot or miss the one you pick by six or seven feet and still end up with a putt at it. It doesn't have to be perfect to work, and remembering that simple fact takes a tremendous amount of pressure off your game.

After an hour or two of practice, you'll see that newfound flexibility in your game. And in the next chapter, you'll also discover just how useful your new skill is—even when you're not playing from grass.

FIVE

Bunkers

The first thing you're going to notice about the standard bunker shot that you'd use for 85 percent of your greenside, basic-lie situations is that it's identical to the high shot we just talked about. The only difference is that you're hitting it from the sand instead of the rough.

Compared to the clinics we run throughout the year, I've actually changed the order of the shots we talk about here in the book. At a clinic, I'd take you from the putting green directly into the bunker to learn trap shots, because you can really illustrate where to hit in relation to the ball by drawing lines in the sand—and the sand is more forgiving of mistakes than the rough is.

I've changed the order here because we're going to talk about more than just the basic high bunker shot. We're going to cover how to read sand conditions in order to make subtle adjustments to the shot you hit, and how to hit other kinds of shots that aren't related to the basic high shot we've been talking about—like intermediate shots from 30 or 40 yards, and full-on fairway-bunker shots.

But before we get to any of that, I think it's important to talk about the psychology of the sand. If you know anything about what I teach, you know how important the mental side is to executing any shot. So many players set themselves up to fail before they even pull a club from the bag because they simply don't believe they can hit a good shot, or they stand over a shot with too many mechanical thoughts running through their head. That's a problem even when the mechanical thoughts match what makes for a good shot. You can imagine what happens when you start thinking about mechanical things that don't work together, or actually work against each other.

If you're coming to this chapter as the average 15- or 20-handicapper, you don't have to feel alone, either. Bunker problems aren't restricted to amateur players. Years ago, Donna Caponi came to me after she had won her second consecutive U.S. Women's Open, in 1970. She told me she was absolutely terrible out of the bunker, and wanted my help to get better. I asked her how a two-time defending Open champion could really be that terrible out of sand, and she had a simple answer. She played every tournament doing whatever she could to avoid hitting the ball into bunkers. She just resolved not to hit into them. She wasn't joking, either. She had never learned the simple technique we're going to talk about here, and she had a rough time hitting consistent shots out of the sand. But after about an hour with me she had it figured out, and she went on to win twenty more times, including two more majors—and earned a place in the World Golf Hall of Fame.

It's easy to joke around about being bad out of the sand, but that problem—whether it's real or in your head—has a huge negative impact on your entire game. Think about what happens if you actually try to play the way Donna did. If your entire game plan is based on fear and avoiding a particular kind of shot, you're going to put a tremendous amount of stress on yourself. It obviously affects your decision-making, and prevents you from hitting certain shots in certain situations.

I sincerely believe that you have to have the positive belief you're going to successfully execute a shot before you can expect to actually do it in real life. It's way, way harder to have that belief if the first step in your mental process is to remind yourself that you just can't go left (or right, or short) on a certain hole because you know you won't be able to get out of the sand.

Now, I'm not saying that avoiding trouble isn't a legitimate part of strategy. But plotting out a course or a hole to avoid out-of-bounds and water is a lot different than trying to avoid something straightforward like a greenside bunker. You obviously don't want to hit a shot into a deep bunker on the short side of the pin—the side where you have less green between yourself and the flag. But a basic bunker shot doesn't need to be such a source of fear.

My argument is that you're going to save yourself a ton of suffering and grinding, mentally and emotionally, if you take the step to get proficient out of the sand. Once you see that it's a pretty easy place to escape, you lose that fear, and you can play so many of your other shots from the fairway and

The bounce on the sole of the wedge trails behind the leading edge and prevents the club from digging into the sand during the shot.

from around the green much less consciously and mechanically. You're free to focus on picking your shot and visualizing it, and staying positive. When I step into a bunker, I feel like I'm about to hit the easiest shot I'm going to have all day. We work so hard on hitting the ball, but on this one, you don't even need to come close to it to hit an OK shot. When it comes to actually hitting the standard greenside bunker shot, most players are overcome with the urge to try to help the ball out of the sand. Most players make a tiny backswing and try to scoop it out, or they take a giant backswing and smash the clubhead into the sand and try to force the ball out.

Neither of those moves takes advantage of the way the clubhead is built.

We're going to get into the nitty-gritty of club anatomy in Chapter 9, but in basic terms, a sand wedge's bounce is designed to trail under the leading edge of the face to keep the club from digging down into the sand. If used properly, the club will skim along the top of the sand, popping a thin layer of sand—and the ball—out of the bunker. All you have to do is get the clubhead moving with the bounce in a place where it can do its job.

When you get into the sand and take that wide stance, bend over, choke down on the grip, and shift your hands forward, everything you're doing is setting you up to rise out of your posture through impact, hang back on your right side, dig the leading edge into the sand, and leave the ball in the bunker—or blade it over the green.

Instead, I want you to stand closer and taller, and angle both of your feet toward the target, as you do for the high shot. Start with your knees flexed slightly, feet about shoulder-width apart, most of your weight on your lead leg, and your ball positioned in the center of your stance. By starting with your weight forward, you're establishing the bottom of your swing arc in a fixed spot, and you're setting up a descending strike on the sand behind the ball. I want your head and shoulders to be as tall as you can make them, and I want them to stay that way throughout the swing. When you angle your feet toward the target, it helps you in the same way it does for the low and high shots: it makes it much easier for you to start with that weight forward and to keep it there throughout the swing. With your feet set too wide and pointed straight at the target line, you'll tend to hang back on your right side.

When you're getting into your stance, you want to dig your spikes into the sand a decent amount—an inch or two—for two major reasons. The first is to get your lower body connected to the ground, so that you can stay stationary through the shot. The process of digging in also lets you get a feel for what's happening just below that top layer of sand. You need to take advantage of that information—whether the sand is hard or soft under the top layer—to preview what the clubhead is going to do when it hits that sand. Generally speaking, the harder the sand, the closer to the ball you need to make contact to hit the shot. You'll get unlucky from time to time and get surprised by the hardness of the sand, but an educated guess is better than no information at all. Don't go too crazy digging in, though. Once your feet get more than a couple of inches below the surface of the sand, you run the risk of hitting it fat.

Now, at this point most teachers would start talking about how far behind the ball they want you to hit to make this shot go. But I find that when you start talking that way it makes the student incredibly ball-conscious. It makes them more likely to crash the club into the sand or scoop at it to try to get the ball in the air.

It's much more effective to focus your attention on where you want the back of the club to strike the sand. That's a trick I learned from an audiotape my dad found of Julius Boros back in the late 1960s. He listened to it and immediately understood why it would help a player get better out of sand, and he kept pestering me to listen. When I listened the first time, I didn't even catch that part of what Julius was saying. But after my dad pointed it out, I went out and hit a few shots from the practice bunker and was astonished at how the ball immediately started coming out high and soft.

To get a sense of what I'm talking about, set up for a 15-yard bunker shot and draw a line three inches behind the ball. Don't pay any attention to the ball, and simply try to hit the back edge of the sole on that line three inches back. The ball will pop straight up into the air. Where the trick comes in really handy is when you've got a longer shot, from more than forty-five feet. On those, you have to hit much closer to the ball, and that can be scary. Set up in the practice bunker for that shot and draw a line a half inch behind the ball. Whack the back edge of the wedge on that line and the ball will pop out, but this time with more drive on it.

To make the swing itself, it's as simple as making a series of guidelines in the bunker. Draw a line from the ball toward your target. Set up so that your feet are aimed on a line to the left of that target line. Keep the face of the club aimed at the hole—along the target line—which automatically sets the face of the club slightly open and exposes more of the bounce. When you swing the club, your path should follow the line your feet are on, from right to left across the ball.

I like to feel the club go back slightly outside my toe line and more vertical, initiated with the thumb and second finger of my right hand. On the downswing, it's going to be a right-hand-dominated shot, with the right hand throwing the clubhead and releasing it through the sand and the left hand basically stopping when it gets back to the ball. The right hand keeps moving through, pushing the club straight down the toe line. You need to keep the feeling of the right palm facing the sky, because that's what keeps the bounce on the bottom of the club aimed at the sand. If you pull your hands and the handle of the club around to the left—which I've seen some instructors teach—you're shrinking the effective area where the clubhead can do its work in the sand, and you're also risking turning the clubhead over. If you let that right hand work up and over the top of the left—so that the right palm is aimed toward the target or toward the ground—you're turning

Set up for a bunker shot with an open stance and both feet angled toward the hole (1). Keep most of your weight on your lead leg and turn the arms and shoulders back in the backswing (2). Focus on hitting the back of the wedge in the sand behind the ball (3), and make a full turn and finish (4). Don't stub the club into the sand.

the digging edge of the club toward the sand. Even if you make decent contact with the sand, you're going to hit a lower, hotter shot. That might work in some specific bad-lie situations—which we'll talk about later—but on a generic sand shot, it's the opposite of what you want.

It's important to mention here that you need to take your stance and establish your ball position first—in the center—before you turn your feet toward the hole. If you set your ball position after you turn your feet, you're going to tend to play the ball too far back. You want to set the ball in relation to the center of your body, not in relation to your toes.

After listening to that tape of Julius Boros, I went and watched him practice out of the sand. It was unbelievable how good he was. Boros, Gary Player, Paul Azinger, and Phil Mickelson are the best I've ever seen from the sand, and they all have differences in how they hit those shots. Gary has always been incredible at controlling the ball out of a variety of lies. He has such good feel for the clubhead that he can manufacture shots in any situation. Azinger is the most dramatically different. He stands far away from the ball, bends over a ton at the waist and in the knees, and uses a super-strong grip. Then he basically recoils the clubhead back out of the sand after impact, almost like he's trying to make a cue ball back up on a pool table. He's a genius with it, and he's remembered for the huge bunker shots he's pulled off to win majors and Ryder Cup matches. Mickelson is simply amazing out of the sand with his 60- and 64-degree wedges, and he does it with more of a forward press than I use. That press matches what he does on his other shots, and it helps him keep a nice, smooth rhythm. He's extremely good on those tight 10-yard bunker shots when the ball needs to get up high and fast. Just like with putting, I'm not going to suggest that my way is the only way to do it. My goal is to give you what I think is the simplest path to hitting consistently solid shots.

Once you have the basics of the setup and swing down, and you've used your feet to get a feel for the sand, you can make simple changes to your setup and where you make contact with the back of the clubhead to change the height of your shots and to account for different sand conditions. You can break sand conditions into two categories: good lies, and less-than-ideal lies. We're going to save the bad lie shots for the next chapter, when we cover trouble shots, but it's important to talk about the different kinds of good lie situations you can face here.

Sand comes in a wide variety of weight and texture, and weather and the way the bunkers are maintained at the course has a huge impact on the overall density of the sand surface. At a place like Augusta National, they have perfectly maintained light sand. On the flat surfaces of the bunker, you'll generally get an excellent lie, with the ball sitting in a slight depression where it landed or rolled. If a course uses a firmer sand, or it's wet or compacted from a lack of use or maintenance, the ball could be sitting up more on top of that firm surface.

The most difficult sand to deal with is exceptionally soft sand, like the kind they use at a U.S. Open. Many times, they bring it in the week before the tournament, and it won't be settled in the bunker. When the ball lands in it, you don't know just how firm the surface is below it. When you hit behind the ball, sometimes you'll get a clean shot that spins, and other times the ball will shoot out and go too far. It's much easier to deal with relatively firm sand that is consistent throughout the depth of the bunker.

The firmness of the sand is going to dictate how closely behind the ball you want to make contact with the sand with the back edge of your wedge. In soft sand, you're going to get more give when the clubhead hits the surface, and you can get away with making contact farther away from the ball. But on firm sand, you want to make contact closer to the ball, so that the wedge doesn't run the risk of bouncing off the harder sand and catching the ball thin. Getting a feel for exactly what kind of shot is necessary for the specific kind of sand you're dealing with is a lot like getting a feel for speed on the green. You have to go out and hit a variety of shots from different sand conditions and start to build up some experience to draw on.

Bunker lies range from a fried egg (left) to buried (center) to ideal, based on how much of the ball is exposed above the sand. In a fried egg lie, the ball is sitting in its own divot, but there's some room around it. In a buried lie, the sand is packed tightly around the ball.

I do want to reassure you about something, though. It's good to know what kind of sand you're dealing with so that you can fine-tune the shot you want to hit, but if you just use the basic bunker shot

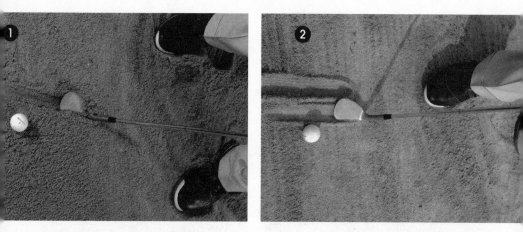

How closely you hit to the ball is determined by the type and firmness of the lie and the kind of shot you want to hit. If you hit two inches behind the ball (1) you'll produce a shot that rolls out more than one where you hit closer to the ball (2).

we've been talking about and hit the back edge of the club two inches behind the ball for every bunker shot, you're going to get pretty good results no matter what sand consistency you're dealing with.

If your lie tells you that you can hit a straightforward high bunker shot, you can start to visualize the shot itself, and pick your very specific landing point—just like we talked about in the last two chapters. A bunker shot is generally going to spin more than the same high shot from grass, so you're actually going to be able to aim closer to the flag and account for less roll than you might for some of the other short-game shots we've been talking about. But that obviously changes when you have a longer, lower shot to hit, and you want to be very specific in your visualization about the landing point versus the point where the ball finishes rolling out.

If you need to hit a bunker shot higher than standard, you can make a few adjustments to your setup to help that happen. First, you can open the clubface, which increases the effective loft of the club. You can also move the ball up in your stance while keeping your hands in the same place relative to your body. When the shaft shifts into a more vertical position or even angles away from the hole—the opposite of a forward press—you're also increasing the effective loft of the clubface.

After you make these setup adjustments, you don't need to do anything

On an uphill (1) or downhill (2) shot, your shoulders and hips should match the plane of the ground at address. The goal is to keep your body perpendicular to the slope. On an uphill shot, avoid leaning too hard into the hill (3), and make your backswing without falling back onto your rear leg (4).

Be sure to accelerate through the finish (5), even if the club buries in the slope. On a downhill shot, don't let your left shoulder drop (6). Swing in line with the slope (7) and prepare for a lower trajectory (8).

special with your swing. In fact, you want to make sure you do the same things that you would on the normal shot and make downward contact with the sand. When the ball needs to get up, your natural urge is going to be to try to help it by lifting your arms and shoulders. That will only increase the risk of bottoming the club out too early and hitting it fat or blading it.

Not every shot you hit is going to be from a perfectly level lie. When you have an uphill or downhill shot, you have to make some adjustments so that you can still make contact in the sand in the right place. The overall concept on any bunker shot is that you want your body to stay as perpendicular to the slope you're on as possible. That means, on an uphill shot, that you're trying to keep your shoulders parallel to the slope, not lean toward it—which would be your natural inclination, in order to try to keep your balance. If you lean into the slope, your tendency will be to dig the club into the sand instead of swinging it through like you want. The same holds true for a downhill shot. You want to match your shoulders to the slope so that the club is still set up to enter the sand in the same place. Let your left shoulder drop too far down—which it wants to do because of gravity—and you'll tend to blade the shot. Exaggerate too much the other way and you'll hang back and scoop it, which produces a fat shot.

As the shot you need to hit gets longer, you transition first to a bigger swing. Notice I said bigger—not faster. I still want your swing to be smooth and rhythmic, with no jerky acceleration. Inside forty-five feet, I'm using my 60-degree wedge to hit the standard bunker shot we've been talking about. After that, I'll often use a 56-degree club with the face more and more square the farther I am from the hole. Make sure that no matter what club you're using, you're making a complete swing to the finish.

When you get to 30 yards or more away from the hole, you're hitting a completely different shot. At that point, you're hitting what amounts to a short pitch shot. Take your 56-degree club—or your gap or pitching wedge, depending on the distance—and (if the lie is good) stand closer to the ball, like you would for a low shot. Choke down on the club two inches and dig your feet in as you would on a standard bunker shot. Instead of exposing the bounce of the club and making contact behind it, make your low-shot swing and hit the ball first. It will come out like a low pitch.

Once you get more than 40 yards away from the flag, you're hitting a full fairway bunker shot. The absolute first key to that shot is understanding

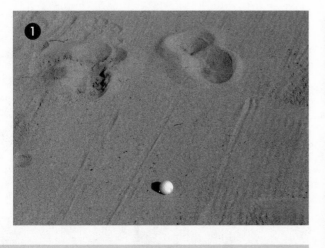

From a fairway bunker, dig your feet in first to make sure you have a stable base (1). Since your feet will be lower, compensate by choking down on the grip (2).

that the lip of the bunker dictates what you do. It's always nice to be able to hit it on the green, but the first goal is to clear the lip and get the ball out of trouble and somewhere safe. Depending on the situation, you might be willing to gamble and cut it close, but for the most part, if you're in a place you don't belong, like a fairway bunker, get back into play and set up for the next shot—even if that means hitting it short of the green to a place where you have a simple chip shot.

Since sand is less stable, you don't want to make a swing with a lot of aggressive leg action. You want to dig your feet in and keep your lower body quiet while making an arms and upper-body swing. This produces less power, so you're generally going to need at least one more club than the yardage would dictate from a fairway lie. But remember, you don't want to mess with the lip in front of you. If it's close, you're going to want to use the more lofted club, even if it leaves you short of your ideal target.

Because you're digging into the sand with your feet, you want to choke down on the handle a full two inches—another factor that will reduce the distance you can hit the shot. If you're able to use more club and still clear the lip, it will also promote a quieter, easier swing, which is ideal out of the sand. You don't need to make any stance adjustments from your standard setup for a shot from the fairway, but you want to make sure you hit the ball

My setup for a fairway bunker shot is the same as my iron setup from fairway grass, but with the ball slightly forward and the clubface slightly open (1). Keep your lower body relatively quiet on the back-swing (2), and be sure to make contact with the ball first before the sand (3). One way to practice this is to use a tee (4) and make sure your divots splash out of the bunker starting beyond the tee (5).

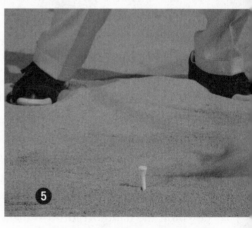

before you hit the sand, even if that means playing the ball slightly back of middle in your stance.

I like to approach every fairway bunker shot as though I'm between clubs. I'll take the longer club, choke down on the handle and hit an intentional fade. By hitting the fade, I increase the loft on the face of the club, which helps clear the lip, and I increase my chances of hitting the ball before the sand. When you're trying to hit a draw, you tend to hang back and swing the hands very aggressively through impact—which often causes you to hit behind the ball. That's fatal on a fairway bunker shot, and almost always results in a fat shot left in the bunker, or one that just trickles out if you're lucky. If anything, you want to err on the side of hitting the ball a bit thin. You can often get away with that, even if it ends up going a bit longer than you intended.

SIX

Trouble Shots

I've spent the first five chapters of this book convincing you that simplifying most of your short-game choices down to two basic options—the low shot or the high shot—is the way to go. And I'm not going to back off of that now.

But (and there's always a "but," isn't there?) when it comes to trouble situations, you need to know how to adapt the basic philosophies we've been talking about here to fit the specifics of what you're facing.

Let me explain what I mean by that.

When I first got out on tour, I had the same repertoire of short-game shots that most people did. I knew how to hit a little bump-and-run shot and a high pitch shot, and when I got into a bad lie situation, I basically opened up the face and tried to chop the ball out the best I could.

But in 1967 or 1968, I was playing a practice round with my friend Dale Douglass before the tour event in Minneapolis. I watched him basically get up and down from everywhere, including some shots from these nasty hardpan lies they had there—and he hit those with a shot I had never seen before. He stood really close to the ball and got the club standing almost vertical, so that the heel was off the ground. That dramatically reduced how much of the bottom of the club was exposed to the ground—so that the club would glide right through with almost no friction. He was able to get the club on the ball regardless of the lie—and in those days, we didn't have 60-degree wedges—and really show me that there were a lot of other shot options out there if you were willing to think beyond the "conventional wisdom." I figured that shot was so good off hardpan it would probably work great off decent lies, too.

I learned this specialty shot from Dale Douglass when we were out on tour together in the late 1960s. Play the ball back in your slightly open stance, and much closer to you than a standard chip (1). The closer ball position pushes the heel of the club up off the ground, leaving less of it to get caught in rough or a divot. The swing itself works just like the low shot from Chapter 3 (2), a push back with the left hand to start and the feeling that you're moving the back of the left hand toward the target on the downswing (3).

We're going to talk about a variety of different shots that are available to hit in trouble situations, but the first point to make is that your job when you come up to your ball and see it in deep grass or a divot or a tough side-hill lie is the same as it was for that basic low or high shot we talked about in the earlier chapters. You need to make an assessment about the quality of the lie and what the realistic possibilities are from it, then pick the shot that provides the best mix of low risk and high reward. That's not always going to be an easy or basic shot, but there are going to be a heck of a lot more situations where you play something low-risk and accept the idea that you're going to be happy just to be on the green and back in position than there are opportunities to try to be a hero.

The most common trouble shots fall into three categories. First, there are varying degrees of rough. The higher and thicker the grass gets, the less control you tend to have over the shot you hit out of that grass. This category also includes shots where your ball might not be in the rough, but it's up against a taller cut of grass, so you have to deal with a backswing that might be restricted to some degree. Second, there are bad lies, like divots or hardpan. Much like the deep rough, you're trying to figure out the most straightforward way to make contact and get the ball out of trouble. Third, there are uneven stance shots—sidehill, uphill, downhill. On those, you have to make some kind of setup adjustment to account for the change in balance you have to have to hit the shot successfully.

I'm not saying there aren't other kinds of trouble shots—things like being up against a tree, or a punch-out shot from the woods. But the shots in the three categories I just described are going to make up a vast majority of the trouble situations you face. Even if you don't experiment with a single one of these shots we're about to talk about, you'll still be ahead if you simply follow along and understand the logic and thought processes behind them.

We'll start by talking about shots from the rough.

Short-game shots from deeper grass have a lot more variables than full iron shots from the rough, and that's mostly because of the speed factor. When you're making a full iron swing, you're generating a lot of clubhead speed, and that speed helps to cut through the rough, especially if we're talking about lighter rough. You obviously have to make some adjustments and pick a different club when the rough gets thicker, but the speed you can generate with a full shot is a huge benefit.

On short-game shots, the amount of speed you can use is hugely dependent on the shot you have in front of you. Sometimes you can use a bunker-style high-shot swing and blast the ball out of the deep rough with a high-speed swing, but what happens if you have a shot where you're in deep grass but only 15 feet from the flag? You need to be able to get the club through the deep grass and get the ball out, but you're not in a position where you can make a giant, full swing—unless you have Phil Mickelson's touch and a 64-degree wedge in your bag. The flop shot he hit on the 15th hole at Augusta National in 2012 might have been the first time somebody tried something that dramatic from those tight lies they have there. It's one of the greatest short-game shots I've ever seen.

After you've made the assessment of your lie that we talked about in Chapter 1 and Chapter 2 and discovered that there's a ton of grass behind your ball, you know you can't get a wedge on the back of the ball cleanly.

That translates into a high shot. We've talked about the basics of a "standard" high shot, which are the same as a bunker shot: weight forward, ball position slightly forward, feet angled toward the target, and the left hand stopped when it gets back to impact.

But when the grass gets thicker, you have to take into account some other factors that don't come into play in light rough, or when you're in the sand. On that standard high shot or bunker shot, many players will lower their hands a bit at address, because that increases the height of the shot. But if you do that from deep grass, you just expose more of the heel and hosel of the club to the grass. You run much more of a risk of getting the hosel snagged, turning the face over and hitting the shot to the left.

For the deep-grass explosion shot, hold the handle a little tighter than normal to stabilize the clubhead as it cuts through the grass, and find a duplicate lie to the one you're facing a few feet away and make some practice swings. If you feel any of that snagging as you come down through the grass, you need to set up with the club taller—not to the point that the heel would be off the ground, but a slightly more vertical shaft setup. When you play the shot this way, with all your weight on your lead leg, a more vertical shaft, and a slightly open clubface, you'll produce enough loft to get the shot to come out high and soft, and the clubhead should glide right through all but the thickest rough.

This definitely goes against the conventional wisdom about playing from rough. I've seen it firsthand at PGA Tour and LPGA Tour events, where tour players play this shot with a very wide stance, low hands, and an extremely open clubface. When you do that, you run the risk of slicing the clubhead—which is laid out flat—right underneath the ball, especially if you let your weight hang back even a touch.

The feel you're looking for is one of standing tall with a taller, more vertical shaft, a slightly open clubface, and weight forward. Pick the club up with the thumb and index finger of the right hand, take it outside slightly on the way back and make a V-shaped swing. Make consistent impact between a half inch and three inches behind the ball (depending on how far you want the shot to go) and you'll be able to consistently get the ball out and onto the green—which is your No. 1 goal. When you get into trouble, get out of trouble and back into position. Bogeys aren't the end of the world. Triples and "others" are.

The setup for a deep-grass shot is the same one that you use for a high or bunker shot (1). Ball position is forward, stance and club are slightly open, and both feet are angled toward the target (2). Take a tighter grip on the handle than normal, and hinge the club quickly on the backswing (3). Stop the left hand and throw the clubhead through impact, and make a full finish in front of you (4). The full finish helps make sure that you're accelerating the clubhead through the grass. Slow it down and it will get stuck.

You can run into issues with rough even if your ball isn't directly in it. Ending up against or near the collar of deeper rough around the green is a common situation, and one that can create some problems if you aren't prepared. Many players use a putter for this shot, but I think there are better choices.

When I have this shot and I'm close to the pin—less than 10 yards away—I'll set up like I would for a putt and use my 54- or 60-degree wedge and hit the equator of the ball with the leading edge of the wedge. Once I get outside that distance, I'll play the ball back in my stance, close to me, and hit a low shot, like we talked about in Chapter 3. The height of the collar I have to deal with behind the ball will determine how abruptly I need to pick the clubhead up on the backswing. If the collar is a normal height, like you'd find on most courses, you don't have to do much to alter your backswing. If you're talking about U.S. Open rough, though, you'll have to make a more vertical swing.

Another option on that shot is to use your hybrid or fairway wood rescue club. Instead of hitting the ball in the middle or just above the middle like you do when you're intentionally blading a wedge, you can make a regular putting stroke and hit the ball squarely. I think it's a great technique, especially if you're not completely comfortable with the bellied wedge shot. It's a very good way to get the ball on the green without much risk. But you do have to go out to the practice green and hit some shots with your hybrid to get a sense for what the ball will do. The only difference in your setup compared to a putt is that the hybrid is a little longer and flatter than a putter. You need to choke down on the handle a couple of inches, and you'll be standing a little bit farther away from the ball than you would on a putt. I use my regular short-game grip—which is the same as my full-swing grip—on that shot, but you could certainly use your putting grip if it's more comfortable.

Another place to use the hybrid club is in deeper grass up to a few feet off the green. When you have a lot of green to work with, and not much deep grass between your ball and the start of the green, you can use your hybrid club from there and hit a shot that pops out of the grass but stays relatively low and immediately starts running when it hits the green. Essentially, you're hitting a low shot, but with your hybrid instead of a wedge. The hybrid is a great club for this shot because it has a wide, flat sole. It will skim

When the collar is right behind your ball and in the way, a wedge will more easily move backward through the taller grass and get back to the ball (1). The setup is the same as a putt, but with the ball shifted slightly back toward the center of the stance (2). The backswing is also similar to that of a putt, and is controlled by the left hand (3). You're trying to keep the clubhead stable through the grass and make contact at or just above the center of the ball with the leading edge of your sand or lob wedge (4). Make sure you don't sole the club at address, or you'll probably hit too low on the ball.

A lower-risk option from the collar is to use a hybrid, which has a broad, flat sole that slides easily through grass (1). Like the bellied wedge shot, the setup is similar to that of a putt (2). You're standing a little farther away from the ball because of the length of the hybrid club, but the swing is the same. Push the clubhead back with the left hand (3) and bring the clubhead back square onto the back of the ball (4). The weight and stability of the hybrid head will keep it on line through the grass. You don't have to worry much about trying to pick it up to avoid the collar.

The hybrid also works well from deeper grass just off the green. The loft on the face is enough to pop the ball out of the grass and get it rolling on the green quickly. Just make sure you can see at least a third of the ball sitting up above the level of the deeper part of the rough.

through the rough without getting snagged, and the low loft on the face is still enough to get the ball up and out—assuming that the ball isn't completely submerged in grass. You can consider this shot if you can see at least a third of the ball sticking up from where the grass starts to get thick.

Divots represent a different kind of problem than deep grass. You have to really pay close attention to the lie and make a judgment about how much of the clubhead you can get onto the back of the ball. The size and shape of the divot is obviously important. If the ball is sitting in a narrow, irregular divot trench, you're going to have to figure out a way to get the face of the club down to the ball. If it's sitting in a wide, relatively shallow divot, you have some other options, including playing it like a standard low or high shot. If you can hit all of the back of the ball cleanly, you can usually hit a low shot, because what the clubhead does after it hits the ball doesn't really matter. That's why it's always easier to hit a shot from the front of a divot than it is from the back.

For these shots, you have to visualize how your clubhead will respond

On a low shot, set up closer to the ball than you would on a putt, with a very upright posture (A). The heel of the club will be just off the ground, both feet will be angled toward the hole. When you hit the shot, you're pushing the club away with the left hand, then moving the back of the left hand straight toward the hole while keeping your posture the same as it was at address (B). You don't want to dip the shoulders to hit the shot, or lift them up to scoop it. The finish is low and down the target line (C). You could simply drop the clubhead and touch the ground after the shot is over.

The low shot is suitable for a strong majority of all the short-game shots you will encounter. It's only when you have a sketchy lie—where the back of the club can't make clean contact on the ball—or when you need to carry an obstacle that a high shot is a better choice.

After visualizing the trajectory of the high shot you're going to hit, align yourself to your landing spot—which should be very specific—not to the hole. The tendency is to subconsciously cheat your stance more toward the flag, which can cause problems when dealing with a shot that has some break after it lands.

When hitting most bunker shots, you want to make a full backswing and follow-through, both at the same speed, and finish high and in front of your body. Your weight starts on your lead leg and stays there throughout the shot.

The setup and swing for a shot from deep rough is the same as your bunker setup and swing—both feet angled toward the hole, weight on the lead leg, and a right-hand dominated swing. The left hand stops while the right hand keeps the face aimed at the sky. You're going to hit behind the ball just like you would out of sand.

To read your putt most accurately, go to the low side of the break—the opposite side of where the apex of the putt's path would be. From that side, it's much easier to see the amount of break and any other green conditions you need to know.

When you walk into your putting stance, set the face of the putter square to your target line while looking at the target (A), not with your head down. After you've set the face, then adjust your stance (B), take a last look at the hole (C), and immediately roll your ball over the spot just in front of the ball on your target line (D).

You can anchor a belly putter in two places, either the center of the stomach (A) or slightly ahead of center. If you anchor it slightly ahead of center, you can make a swing that still reaches the ball on a relatively descending blow. The backswing (B) works the same as it would with a standard putter, controlled with the left hand. The anchored part of the shaft keeps the putter swinging on a controlled arc (C), so the clubhead has to keep moving upward after impact (D). Ball position is very important. If you let it creep too far forward, you'll make glancing contact, almost like you would if you topped a shot with an iron.

The shot you can hit is primarily determined by the kind of divot you find yourself in (1). You can see how a club angled more upright (2) fits more easily into a deeper, narrow divot and can pop a ball out (3). When you play the club more flat and square, the broad sole catches the edges of the divot and can send the club offline (4).

when it hits the irregular edges of the divot. If you turn the clubhead open, you're creating a wide, flat area at the leading edge. If the divot is narrow and deep, that flat area probably won't be able to get down to the ball. This is where Dale Douglass's shot is so valuable. By getting the club in a much more vertical position, to where the toe is on the ground and the heel is in the air, you're creating a very narrow footprint for your club. It can fit right down into the divot, and you still have a wide part of the face to make contact with the ball. The first time I tried it, it was shocking how easily the ball

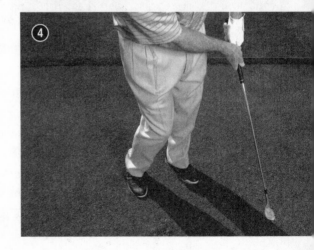

To play a shot from a divot, set up in your low-shot stance, with the ball back in your stance but closer to you (1). This will set the clubhead so that it's up on its toe. Make a steep swing that moves along the target line back and through (2), and swing the clubhead through impact with a firm, flat left wrist (3). Don't try to scoop the ball out of the divot or otherwise let the left wrist break down.

popped right out of the divot. You want to use your most lofted wedge for this shot, and to give yourself plenty of room for the ball to run out. It's going to come out without much backspin.

If the lie is really nasty, and you're sitting down in a sand-filled hole, you could consider hitting a high shot using the technique we talked about in Chapter 4. You're really playing it like a bunker shot and exploding it out of the bad lie. It's a much higher-risk shot, and one I've only really tried a handful of times in my entire PGA Tour career. If the lie is that bad, you're usually better off playing something much lower-risk, even to the point where you're not really going for the flag or the green. Take your punishment and get into a position where you can try to get up and down with the next two shots. If you hit the explosion shot and catch it wrong, you're going to blade the ball over the green, and you could make a big, big number.

Hardpan or other super-firm lies can be tricky, but I don't think they present as much of a problem as divots do. When the ground is that firm, you're going to have a clean look at the back of the ball. That usually dictates a low shot, unless you have some kind of obstacle in front of you. The only thing you have to make sure to do on a hardpan shot is to avoid hitting the ground before you hit the ball. When the club hits the ground first, it will rebound off the firm surface and hit high on the ball. If you make sure to keep your weight forward, you run much less risk of hitting behind the ball.

When you're on an uphill or downhill slope, you're really trying to do the same thing on both shots. You're trying to recreate a balanced equilibrium in your setup position, so that you're effectively hitting from a level lie. You're trying to match the slope.

On a downhill shot, your weight is going to shift forward, and you want to tilt your shoulders so that they match the angle of the hill. If you tried to maintain your true upright balance for the shot, your weight would favor your back foot, and you'd be set up with your left shoulder higher than your right. Those factors would pretty much guarantee that you'd crash the clubhead into the slope before it got to the ball—producing a topped or bladed shot. I also make it a point to stand slightly closer to the ball on a downhill shot, because the upright shaft helps produce a little bit more loft.

Your mind-set needs to be similar on an uphill shot—just a mirror image. You still need to have more weight on your lead leg than you do on your back leg, but you have to try to set your shoulders level with the slope and keep yourself from leaning too far into the hill—which, again, would cause you to crash the club into the ground instead of swinging it along the slope. You also have to be careful about letting your weight shift too far back with gravity, which will pull your right shoulder lower than your left.

On both shots, you need to keep the same narrow stance we talked about in the high-shot chapter, because you have much more control over where your weight is established over your feet, and where you transfer it during a shot. From a wide stance, your tendency is to get your weight very centered, and then leave it there throughout the swing. It's extremely hard to get your weight onto that lead leg when your stance is too wide.

Even the best players we teach are surprised when we show them just how much the trajectory and quality of a shot can change based on whether it's played from an uphill, downhill, or level lie. Unless you're very careful with your setup and where you set your weight, you're probably not going to hit a very good shot. When you're playing from an uphill lie, the slope

The goal on a downhill shot is to set your stance so that you match the slope. My shoulders—and the plane line I'm holding in front of me represented by the club—match what you would see if I was on a flat surface (1). When I set up on the low shot, all of my weight is on my lead leg (2). The right is there just for stability.

For the downhill shot, my stance is narrow, shoulder-width apart, and my ball position is in the center or slightly back of center (1). My backswing stays long and works along the angle of the slope, while my weight stays on my lead leg (2). I don't help the ball up in any way—I just let the loft on the club do the work (3) and push the back of my left hand toward the hole into a free finish out in front of me (4).

automatically creates more height on any shot you hit, and you then have to account for it when you visualize the shot and the size of the swing you're going to use. Shots from downhill lies are naturally going to come out lower and with more run. That has to be a part of the equation when you visualize where you want to go.

One last, important thing to stress about all of these shots is that the setup and ball position guidelines I've given are for "standard" shots. In the real world, I'm always making slight adjustments to my ball position or my shaft position to produce a different trajectory. My ball position can change an inch or two up or back, depending on whether I want to make the shot go higher or lower. Generally speaking, the farther back you play the ball, the more forward the shaft will lean and the lower the shot will go. If you adjust the ball position forward, or play the ball in the middle but lean the shaft more neutral or even slightly back, you'll produce more height.

If you're looking for a chart with specifics on how much higher or lower

Players struggle with uphill shots when they let the gravity of the slope push them back down the hill, so that the right shoulder is lower than the left (1). That produces a hang-back backswing (2) and a flip move on the through swing that usually bottoms out behind the ball (3).

To hit a good uphill shot from 30 yards and in, set your balance and your shoulders to match the slope (1), while making sure that your weight continues to favor your lead leg (2). Notice how both of my feet are angled toward the target. My shoulders stay level during the backswing (3), and my weight stays on my lead leg throughout the shot (4).

each adjustment in ball position or shaft angle will produce, I can't help you there. It's a matter of feel and experimentation. The best way to get good at these shots is old-fashioned practice and experimentation. Start with the "standard" shots we talk about here, then see what a little modification in ball position does for you. You'll know which variations really work for you, and when you've gone too far.

SEVEN

Mental Game

We've spent a lot of time talking about technique over the last few chapters, but if you know anything about my teaching philosophy, you know that I believe mechanics are secondary to what you think and see.

Now, that's an easier thing to grasp in putting, because you really aren't making any decisions other than picking your line. At that point, you're simply visualizing your line, keeping a positive, clear mind and rolling your ball. (And if you need a refresher on just how to do that in putting, you can turn to Chapter 10.)

In the short game, you're dealing with the added dimension of high or low versus a putt rolling along the ground, and the added complication of variable lies. You have more decisions to make, and the shots you are required to hit have some more moving parts. Because of that, you've got more room to make the wrong decision, and the potential for more time to let negative thoughts override what you're trying to do.

Does all of this mean that your mental process needs to be fundamentally different for a short-game shot than it does for a putt?

Not at all.

I want you to see a scoring-game shot from within 30 yards of the green as an extension of what you would do on the green itself. The foundation of a solid scoring game—whether it's on a chip, a pitch, a bunker shot, or a putt—comes from visualization, routine, and confidence.

Let's take those one at a time.

The process of visualizing the shot you want to hit starts from the moment you walk up to the ball and start making a decision about hitting a low shot or a high shot. It's really the first part of your pre-shot routine. Once you've made the choice, you need to get really specific about what you want the shot to look like when you hit it.

When I see a shot I'm going to hit, I see it exactly as if I was watching a video replay of it on television—from the exact spot on the green where it will land, to the way it checks (or doesn't) when it lands, to how it rolls out.

Just like with a putt, the most important part of the shot is the last third. It's where the ball is slowing down and getting influenced the most by the slope of the green. On shorter chip shots, I'll walk up onto the green and go through the same reading routine that I would use on a putt to get a really clear visual of what the ball will be doing on that last third. I'll go to the low side of the break—the side opposite the shot path's apex—and look at it from down there. Equating that with the face of a clock, if the ball is at 6 and the hole is at 12, for a shot that will break right to left, the apex of the break would come on the 3 side of the clock face, and the low side of the break would be on the 9 side.

On every short-game shot—from a low shot 20 feet from the hole to a 20-yard bunker shot—you want to pick, whenever possible, the exact spot on the green (or the fringe, in some cases) where you want the ball to land. That landing point will then become the focus of your visualization routine, and the point to which you align yourself when you're ready to hit the shot. As you'll see in the next chapter, which discusses drills, going through the process of picking that spot—and then practicing hitting to it when it's marked off on the practice green—is terrific training in both seeing the result of the shot and comparing it to what you visualized, and working on the ability to actually hit to the spot you chose.

The spot I pick when I visualize the shot I hit is extremely specific. I'm talking drop-a-quarter-on-the-green specific. The benefit of picking such a specific spot is the same benefit you get when you pick a spot to roll the ball over on a putt. When my son Ron is working with a player on putting, he'll have them roll a ball over a spot an inch in front of the ball and immediately call out if they liked the stroke or not. They quickly see that a ball that isn't hit exactly the way they want can still turn out well. It helps take away the pressure to be perfect, and lets them focus on the process, instead of being so worried about the outcome. The same is true on a short-game shot. You can pick your exact spot, miss it slightly, and still get a good result. By picking the spot, you're giving your mind really specific information to use for visualization, and you're giving yourself something concrete to aim to and play for. To me, it's the difference between parking your car in the garage in the middle of the day and trying to do it blindfolded.

You might think that it's silly to go through the process of visualizing an extremely specific result on a shot if you aren't a particularly good short-game player. The thinking goes that if you can't hit a shot very consistently, what does visualizing a good result really matter to the outcome?

I'm here to tell you that it makes a huge difference. Ever since I read the book *Psycho-Cybernetics*, by Maxwell Maltz, in the late 1960s, I've used visualization during every round I've played. I hit every short-game shot with the idea that I'm trying to make it. I see it rolling into the hole. Of course, I don't make every one, but the process of visualizing the shot rolling in— and the extra focus I put on that last third of the roll—helps me see the best place for that shot to end up if it doesn't go into the hole. And that's the part of the process that can be so valuable for the 10- or 20-handicap player. You want to visualize every shot going in—after all, you can't do something consistently if you can't see yourself doing it—and get the benefit of understanding which quadrant around the hole is the best place to leave yourself an easy putt.

I can't tell you how many times I've played pro-am rounds with amateur players in which we'll get together beforehand and discuss the ideal shot for a given situation, only to see the player go on to hit the shot in the exact worst place it could go. In a lot of cases, the worst place to be is very obvious. If there's a big drop-off behind the hole, it behooves you to be careful about knocking the shot too far by and down that drop-off. But the dangers are sometimes subtle, too. Augusta has an example like that on every hole. They place the pins in some really difficult places, and getting close to the hole isn't necessarily the best place to be if you're left with a three-footer with a nasty sidehill break. The best place to end up—if not in the hole—might be 10 feet away, but in a place where you have a straightforward uphill look at a putt.

When it comes down to it, quality in the short game means consistency. It means hitting the shot you want to hit, time after time. That consistency comes from having a good routine—from reading the situation to visualizing the shot to setup—for every shot, no matter what the stakes are. And obviously, golf isn't played in a vacuum. The chip shot or bunker shot you have in front of you usually means something. You're trying to save par, win a hole, or post a score. Anybody can pull another ball out of the pile at the practice green and hit one up close to the hole when it doesn't count for anything.

What we're trying to do here is develop a straightforward, simple technique for low shots and high shots, pick the right shot for the situation, and come up with a routine for the entire process that becomes automatic no matter what the situation is. If you have a solid routine, it becomes a self-perpetuating thing. It's something you can fall back on and use as a focus point instead of getting caught up in the consequence game—that is, thinking about what happens if you miss. In the final round of the 1970 PGA Championship, I hit my approach shot into the water on the 13th hole and was left with a 40-yard pitch shot off hardpan. I hadn't felt very good over the approach shot, but that pitch was a different story. I couldn't wait to hit it, and I went through my normal routine—even with a hostile crowd around me pulling for Arnold Palmer. I hit it to three inches to save bogey, and I went on to win the tournament.

I'm not suggesting you take the routine I'm about to describe and copy it exactly for your own. It's more important to understand that each part of my routine has a purpose, and that there's nothing extra in there. You can pick and choose the parts that work for you, as long as you understand the overall idea that shorter is better than longer, and that you need to effectively bridge the space between reading and seeing the shot and getting into position to hit it without giving yourself time to overthink or tense up.

After I've gone through the process of picking the shot and the club I'm going to use and visualizing the path that I want the ball to take, I'll pull the club and make some light practice strokes to feel what the club is going to do as it moves through the grass. All the different varieties of grass—bermuda, bent, kikuyu—will influence the club differently. Bermuda and kikuyu will tend to snag the clubhead on a slower swing, even in light rough. That's going to strongly influence the shot you choose to play, and probably push you toward hitting a high shot with more clubhead speed. Bent grass will let the clubhead slide through quickly if it's cut tightly, or if you're swinging in the same direction as the grain.

If I have a shot from the fairway, I'll make those practice strokes six inches inside the ball. But from the rough, I'll go a few feet away, in grass that looks the same as the lie I have, so I don't disturb the ball with my practice swing and get a penalty. Through this process, I'm also paying close attention to the feel in my feet, and whether I'm sinking down into the grass or at the lowest point, where the actual ground is. That gives me information about how much grass I have under my ball, and how deep I can swing before hitting dirt. The same process holds true in the bunker, where your feet give you lots of information about the firmness of the sand. You obviously can't ground your club in there, so your feet are your best source of information.

At this point in my routine, I've already pictured what the shot is going to do. I see in my mind how high it's going to fly, and where it will land and run out. Now I'm connecting that visual to my practice swing, and I'll think about the movement of my left hand toward the hole on a low shot and the release of my right hand for a high shot or a bunker shot. After two or three brisk practice swings for feel, I'll step into my stance, take one look at the target, look down at my ball and lift the club slightly as I waggle so that I'm not frozen over the ball. On a low shot, I'll make a slight forward press and make my swing. On a high shot, I'll just lift the club and keep my hands in the same position relative to the ball at address, because that's where I want the left hand to stop in the swing. Then I'll finish my routine and let the shot happen.

My routine doesn't change, no matter what the situation might be. You've probably seen a player in the last few holes of a tour event take a lot more time over a short-game shot that he or she absolutely needs to get close. That's a mistake. Routines work because they're just that—routine. Taking extra time over a shot might make sense intuitively, because you want to make sure you're ready, but going slower just gives you more time to second-guess yourself and to get more nervous. The more time you leave between your read and the shot itself, the more you disconnect from the read. You're less fresh, and you're getting tighter by the second.

Now, we're all human, so I'm not going to try to tell you that a great routine is going to block out every negative thought that you're ever going to have on the golf course. We all go through ups and downs and have good and bad stretches of confidence. Look at what's happened to Tiger Woods. He went a decade standing over every putt knowing it was going in the hole. Now that he's missed a few, he's thinking more about his stroke and wondering how to get it back. He's thinking about getting from point A to point B, instead of just letting it go and trusting all that skill and experience he's built up.

The fact that this happened to arguably the best player of all time is proof that it can happen to anybody.

But if you can stick to your routine and convince yourself to stay positive, the lows aren't going to be quite as low. Even if your short-game technique is a work in progress, I want you to go out the next time and approach each shot from 30 yards and in as a shot that you're looking forward to hitting. You can even sell yourself on the idea that you're excited to try the low and high shots we've been talking about here, and that you want to see how well you can pick them up. You can definitely feed off even one positive result.

One of the best side effects of committing to the idea that every short-game shot is either low or high is the clarity it gives you in your decision-making process. When you're in a position to pick one shot or the other, the choice is simple, and you're never faced with hitting an in-between shot. You're going to see a huge surge in confidence, simply because you're going into every shot with a black and white plan. There are only two shots to practice, and your ability to judge the lie and the conditions around the green is going to improve dramatically as you get a little experience. When you feel like you're hitting the right shot for the situation, you're able to clear your head of a lot of doubt and negativity that is a regular part of so many players' pre-shot experience.

If something does go wrong—and it does from time to time for all of us—try to remember two important things. First, the golf course isn't the place to be consumed with mechanics. When you're playing, you're going to have the most success if your swing thoughts are confined to a single trigger idea—like left hand to the hole for a low shot, or stopping the same left hand for a high shot. Once it gets beyond that, you're just confusing yourself and making it harder to make a smooth, relaxed swing. It's impossible to think of a long checklist of moves you want to make—even on a motion as simple as a putting stroke. It's fine to keep track of the misses so you can go back during your practice time and work out some of the problems, but on the course, you need to stick to your single swing thought, see your shot, and continue to let it go.

You'll also do well if you can learn how to let the anger over a bad shot come and then go just as quickly as it came. Hey, I'm not going to try to tell you that you're not supposed to get mad if you blade one over the bunker or chunk a chip shot. It's natural to feel that flash of anger, and to express it.

But you need to blow off that steam without blaming yourself or calling yourself names—or letting one bad shot pull you into a series of them. I'm sure you've had a day where you've three-putted a couple of times the first few holes, and by the fifth or sixth hole you've convinced yourself that it just isn't your day. Beware of that type of thinking. Your mind is powerful, and thinking that way pretty much determines that the rest of the day *will* go that way.

The short game works the same way. If you get in a bad place in the bunker on the first hole and hit a poor shot, you can look forward to your next chance to try a sand shot, or you can tell yourself that you're a terrible sand player and spend the rest of the day dreading the thought of ending up in the sand.

Which way do you think is easier on your mind—and more fun?

I can't stress enough how beneficial it is to embrace the idea that the short game is an exciting, creative part of the game where you get the chance to hit shots that don't take any superhuman strength or decades of special practice. A good pitch shot counts the same as a 320-yard tee shot, or a towering 200-yard approach shot with a 5-iron, and you don't have to be a tour player to hit it.

EIGHT

Practice and Drills

From the time I was a kid, creating all kinds of short-game shots on the holes that were basically in my front yard, a vast majority of my "practice"—whether it was short game or long game—came from putting myself in situations and experimenting to find the best result.

That sense of curiosity, challenge, and pure fun is missing from a lot of players' practice time now. Getting better might be serious business for you, and that's OK, but I can tell you that incorporating some more dynamic and enjoyable routines and games into your practice—instead of grimly hitting big buckets of balls like a robot—will give you much better results.

After we finish a Stockton Golf clinic or individual lesson, many of the students will come up at the end and ask what kind of practice "program" they should follow when they get back home. I'm sure many of them are hoping to get a handout showing them exactly how many low shots, high shots, sand shots, and trouble shots they need to hit—and from what lies—to get X percent better by the end of the month.

That's just not the way the boys and I approach the game.

If you read my putting book, you know that I believe that putting is more art than science. I think the short game has a touch more science than that, but it's still mostly art. My goal here is to give you a series of simple drills that are all designed to do the same thing—get you to learn the feel of the few different shots you need, and to get through the mechanical learning process and to that feel and shot-selection process as quickly as possible.

At the end of the day, I want you to be able to pick the shot you're going to hit, let the simple setup and swing basics click in almost without a thought, and then direct all of your attention to seeing, feeling, and making the shot you want to hit happen.

A few players will take one of our clinics and promptly go out with that large bucket and hit a hundred short-game shots in a row from the same exact place on the green. Not only is that not helpful, it's actually counterproductive. Nothing about that helps you improve the most important part of the short-game process, which is seeing the shot you need to hit.

In the entire time I've played competitive golf, I've never hit a ton of balls. And that's not because I've always had a good short game. I divide my practice time into two segments—what I'm doing at home to work on my game, and what I'm doing at a tournament site to get ready for a round. Those two things aren't remotely the same—in fact, I'd almost hesitate to call my pre-round routine practice. The only thing they have in common is that they're both designed to enhance feel.

Let's talk about the off-course part of practice first, since it's going to be the place you'll probably be spending more time right now trying to digest some of the ideas we've been talking about in this book.

The first step is to get comfortable with the shots themselves. The drills I'm going to show you here will go a long way toward helping you with the feel you need for each of the shots. Start your practice session using one of the drills for each of the low, high, and sand shots, and go through the drills several times. For example, hit three or four one-handed low shots, just to reinforce the feeling of the clubhead staying stable and low through impact, then simulate two or three high shots with your open right hand. I don't want you to go overboard and do drills for an hour or an hour and a half, because it's important to transition to seeing and hitting real shots—that's where the real improvement comes.

At the practice green, pick three flags that require a variety of shots. Instead of lugging that big bucket of balls over, use a limited number of balls. Think about the basics we talked about for the low shot, and pick the hole that you see as most receptive to a low shot. Hit it up there. Next, choose the hole that is best suited to a high shot, and do the same. Go through the same process with another ball or two, then judge your results. Pick up the balls and go through the process again, but from a different spot. A vast majority of Phil Mickelson's short-game practice comes from using this technique and four balls. He's learning to feel different shots to the different pins.

When you look at your results, take in more than just how far you ended up from the hole. When you hit these shots, you should be reading the last third of them just as you would a putt. There are places around almost every hole—unless it's dead flat—that are better to be putting from than others. You're trying to leave yourself with a flat or uphill putt, not something with a lot of downhill or sidehill break.

You can also take note if you have a predominant kind of miss. Most players stand too square to these shots, and if they hit ten of them, seven end up to the right of the target for just that reason. You're building in your feel for distance, but also assessing your direction control.

The more specific you are about your target and the more you expect to hit a good shot, the better your results are going to be. There's nothing wrong with expecting to make your short-game shots. I can tell you that when I'm hitting a little low shot or a pitch, I'm trying to hole every one. When you watched a player like Raymond Floyd hit a chip shot, there's no question he was surprised and annoyed when he didn't hole out from a good lie off the green. He had a better chance to make one from 30 feet with his wedge than he did with his putter. That's a powerful weapon to have in your game.

As I said previously, I've never been a big proponent of hitting tons of balls. The reality for a lot of us is that we don't have a huge amount of time to practice. If you're going to devote a couple of days a week, an hour at a time, to range practice, that's an impressive commitment.

If you do have an hour to practice, I want you to get the most out of that time. It's not about how many balls you hit, but how much you learn from the ones you do hit. Think about the shot breakdown of your last round. How many drivers did you hit? 12? 14? How many fairway wood shots or hybrid shots? Now compare that to the average number of short-game shots and putts you hit in a given round. I bet you hit at least fifty, when you add up putts, chips and pitches, bunker shots, and other less-than-full wedge shots. To me, that indicates that you should be spending at least half of the practice time you get on those shots.

When you actually get to the course before a tee time, your strategy has to change from practice and skill development to touch and feel. Standing in the short-game practice area 20 minutes before your tee time is not the time to be experimenting with a new bunker technique or chipping club that you've never tried before. The time before your round is meant to be spent loosening up to get your body ready to go, and to access the touch and feel you've been working on during practice times. Go around the practice green and hit a few shots just to see how the clubhead reacts to the grass conditions on the course that day. You can get a feel of how wet or dry it is, and how your shots are rolling out when they hit the green. You're calibrating your feel and distance control subconsciously.

I'd go so far as to say that if you only have twenty minutes before your tee time, you're better off hitting *no* practice shots, or very few. Instead of rushing around trying to solve some swing problem, relax and make your game plan for the day and get a sense for what the wind is doing. Make some practice swings with no ball, to get your back loose, and commit to playing with a clear mind. You might have heard this story before, but it's a good one to retell. I was at the Masters one year, and I ran into Byron Nelson. I had six or seven things I was working on in my swing, and I asked him how he kept all that straight in his head when he played. He told me that in 1945, when he won all those tournaments in a row, he played the entire season with one single swing thought. He loosened up on the range for twenty minutes and went out and played. That was it. He didn't hit balls after, and he didn't spend a bunch of time on the practice tee. He had one thing, and he went with it.

At that point in the story, everybody always asks me what Byron's swing thought was.

I don't know. I didn't ask because it didn't apply to me.

DRILLS

When we're running a Stockton Golf clinic or individual lesson, we use drills a little bit differently than many other teachers do. Similar to what we've been talking about in terms of overall practice, I'm not in favor of you going on and hitting hundreds of balls in a mindless way. These drills are designed to get you feeling the right motions and seeing your short-game shots—and they're designed to get you transitioning to real golf shots as soon as possible.

Take some of the drills in each category we're going to talk about here—low shots, high shots, sand shots, and, as a bonus, putting—and try them a few times at the beginning of your practice session. Then hit some real shots to link the feel in the drill to the feel in "real life." If all you ever do is work on the drill, you're going to get really good at the drill—not the real shot.

Low-Shot Drills

Our short-game clinics start with a putting lesson, then transition to a low shot just off the green. And the first thing we have a player do is experiment hitting one-handed low shots with just the left hand. (A left-handed player would do the opposite, and practice with just the right hand.)

If you struggle to hit chip shots, it's probably because you have an over-active right hand. You're trying to help the ball up by scooping the right hand through impact. As soon as you try to hit one-handed shots with just the left hand, you're going to get an awkward surprise if you try to help the ball up in the air. The left hand by itself can't support the club when you let the wrist break down, and by break down, I mean bend upward at the top of the wrist.

After a few awkward swings, you'll soon automatically sense a better way to move the club. You'll push it back with the left hand, and swing it through with a solid left wrist and let the loft on the clubhead do the work of shooting the ball in the air. The one hand on the club also helps you feel the weight of the clubhead, and simply let it move down through the bottom of the swing and brush the ground just in front of the ball.

The one-handed drill is also a great way to get control over the size and speed of your low-shot swing. It's easier to move the club with one hand when you make a smooth, controlled swing with a gentle change of direction at the top of the backswing. Pulling or shifting the club fast, or jerking it into the downswing will just make it harder to make solid contact. All of these things are great reminders when you get to the real deal.

My swing feel on a low shot is not too different than it would be for a putt of the same length. When I move the putter, I obviously have no thought of the ball getting up in the air. From a good lie around the green, I'm not think-ing about how to get the ball up in the air on a low shot, either. The ball just gets in the way of the clubhead, like it does on a putt, and my left hand goes straight at the hole. My setup and ball position take care of the rest.

Set up in the standard low-shot stance, with the ball off the right big toe, feet hip-width apart, and toes turned toward the target (1). Holding the club with just the left hand, push the clubhead back slowly and smoothly (2), and let the weight of the clubhead help the transition to the downswing. Keep the back of the left wrist flat (3) and let the loft on the clubhead produce the height in the shot, with your left hand leading and going through low.

The one-handed drill is designed to show you exactly how the club should move, even when you end up with two hands on the club (1). Push the clubhead back with just the left hand (2), add the right hand, and you'll be in perfect position (3).

Another way to get instant feedback on your low-shot technique is to extend the butt of the club with a broken shaft— or take another club and turn it around so that you're holding the grips together but the other shaft extends back away from the ball. When you make a swing with the extended grip and your left hand goes straight at the hole without breaking down, the extended shaft will stay away from your upper body, because the shaft will basically be forward pressed throughout the shot. When you let your right wrist scoop at the ball and the left wrist responds by breaking down, the extended shaft will bang off of your left side.

If you try to flip your hands at the ball to help it up in the air, you're reducing the arc of your swing, and you'll have to dip your shoulders and change your posture to hit the ball. Even if you can somehow dip the exact right amount, you have to catch the ball at the exact time the clubface is square to the target and flush on the ground to hit a decent shot. That's a hard way to be consistent. Hubert Green was a magician at it, but he had world-class hands.

Hit a half dozen balls with an extended shaft and you'll quickly learn to make low-shot swings while keeping the right hand completely out of it—and your consistency will improve immediately.

High-Shot Drills

If the goal for the low-shot drills was to reinforce the idea that the right hand stays out of the swing and the left hand moves toward the hole without breaking down, the goal for the high shot is the complete opposite. Here, we're trying to develop the feel for the right hand throwing the clubhead aggressively through impact.

To fight the common tendency to lift up with the left shoulder (or drop the right), try the left-hand drill with your right hand across your chest and holding on to your left shoulder. This will make you more conscious of your left shoulder position and help keep it level.

Many players get sidetracked over what it means to throw the clubhead. They'll either smash the club into the ground, or turn it over so that the leading edge actually digs more into the ground. The concept is actually as simple as it sounds. Stand in your setup without a club, with your arms extended in front of you and a ball in your right hand. Now make a full, slow swinging motion and throw the ball up in the air to a target 10 feet in front of you. To make the ball go up in the air, your palm has to stay

By extending the shaft from the end of your wedge (1), you can give yourself a physical reminder to keep the back of the left wrist firm through the shot. When the left wrist doesn't break down (2), the extended shaft stays out in front of the body all the way through the shot (3). If the left wrist bends, the shaft will crash into your torso.

facing the sky—which is exactly where it needs to be when you hit a high shot.

If you make that same motion and throw the ball toward the ground, you've turned your hand over with the wrong kind of wrist action.

As with the low shot, how you set up to the ball goes a long way toward how well you'll hit it. The key to a high shot is setting up with a slightly open stance, turning your feet toward the target, and swinging on an upright plane along the line of your feet. You can use three guide sticks—club shafts also work great for this—to give yourself a visual frame of reference when you practice these shots.

First, set your feet slightly open to the target and lay one guide stick in front of them. Then set the second stick parallel to the first, on the far side of the ball. Stick the third stick into the ground near the back end of the stick that's in front of your feet, and slightly to the inside. When you set your feet to the first stick, the one that's right in front of you, aim the clubface directly at the

The feel you want on a high shot is that of your right hand coming through with the palm facing the sky, as though you were tossing a ball to a spot 10 feet in front of you (1). If you let the hand roll over (2), you reduce the effective loft on the club and expose the leading edge of the wedge to the ground.

target. Because your stance is open, you will have automatically opened the face just the right amount for the shot. The third stick prevents you from pulling the club inside on the takeaway into a too-flat position behind you.

I like the guide sticks because they're a vivid reminder of where you need to be in your setup. Even tour players get a little bit off in their setup from time to time without noticing. Make three or four practice swings with no ball to get a feel for the position of the vertical stick, then hit three or four shots standing in the guide station.

This third drill is less of a drill and more of a visualization trainer—and it really works with any of the shots in this chapter. Pick a random high shot at the short-game practice area and pick the exact landing spot that you think will put your ball in the hole. Drop a small Stockton Golf Ring on your landing spot, and then take two or three balls and practice trying to land them in the ring. Of course, the landing itself is just one part of the challenge. You can judge by where the ball rolls out if you picked the right

Guide clubs can help you set up for the high shot. Your stance should be open to the target by about 30 degrees, and once you've done this, drop one guide club in front of your feet (1). The second guide club is parallel to the first, on the far side of the ball. Set the clubface square to the target line, and swing the club up vertically so that it stays in front of the third guide club (2), which is stuck in the ground just behind and to the inside of the first guide stick. That vertical swing plane, along with the open clubface, produces height on the shot.

landing spot. If you're consistently long or short even when you land in your target area, you'll know that your visualization and landing-point selection skill are what need work, not your technique.

Another great way to use a target ring is to drop two or three of them on the green and practice hitting the same club to each of the rings, which will force you to change the trajectory and distance on each shot. You can also use one ring and change your position up and back, hitting one club or a variety of clubs to land the ball inside the target circle.

I find that using the circles really helps average players pick and visualize the shot without getting discouraged or skeptical about hitting a smaller target. You could put a quarter or a dime out there and try to hit it, but I don't know how much good feeling you're going to get if you're never successful.

Sand Drills

To get a feel for how a change in where the back of the club enters the sand changes the trajectory and distance of your bunker shots, stick two tees in the ground behind a ball in the practice bunker, one an inch behind and another two inches behind. Then make a series of practice swings next to the ball and tees, concentrating on hitting the back edge of the club's bounce—not the leading edge—parallel with first the closest tee and then the one farther back.

After two or three swings in which you just splash sand, hit two real shots, making contact with the sand an inch behind, and then two inches behind. You'll notice that the shots where you made contact closer to the ball will go higher and longer, and land with more backspin. This drill illustrates very simply two sand shots at

Connect your practice to the course by visualizing the landing spot for your shot, dropping a guide ring, and judging your results. Miss the ring and you need help with your swing. Hit the ring but leave it far from the flag and you need work on your visualization and landing-spot judgment.

the opposite ends of the spectrum. Once you've had a chance to get the feel for the shot, you'll have an almost infinite number of options from the sand, and you'll be able to let the situation and the lie dictate the best choice.

Draw a line straight to the hole with the foot line open and the path of

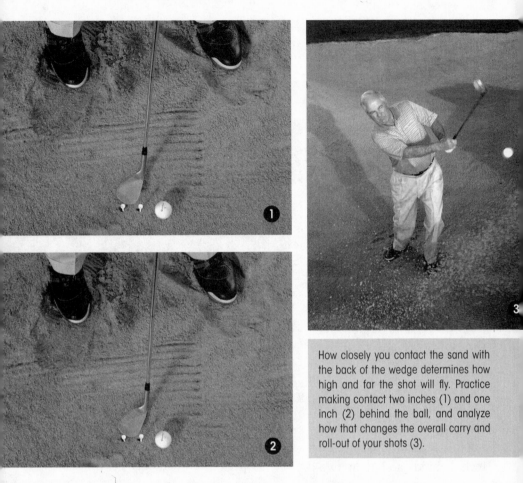

How closely you contact the sand with the back of the wedge determines how high and far the shot will fly. Practice making contact two inches (1) and one inch (2) behind the ball, and analyze how that changes the overall carry and roll-out of your shots (3).

the club square to that foot line. Set the clubface so that it's square to the target. Slightly open to your foot line and path. Most people set the face way too open because they're trying to get it up. They get a wide stance, turn the right foot out, hit a million miles behind it and try to help it up, and they hit the ball three feet—or 40 yards.

I've been using the rake drill in the bunker for more than thirty years, because it's simple and effective. People can't believe how easy it is to get the ball out of the sand when they get the bounce of the club sliding instead of digging. Simply dig a trench in the bunker and bury a rake so that there's about an eighth of an inch of sand over the handle. Set the ball on top of the buried handle, and then set up to the shot with your standard bunker stance.

When you hit the shot, the buried wooden (or plastic) handle won't let

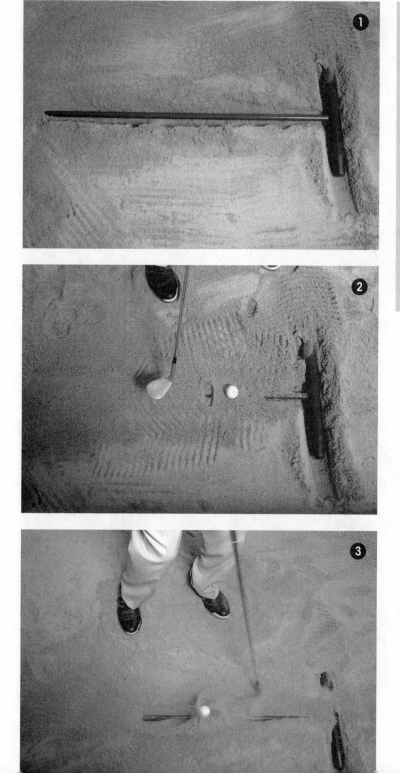

Bury a bunker rake an eighth of an inch below the sand (1) and practice hitting shots from directly on top of the handle (2). The wood just under the surface of the sand prevents the clubhead from digging in too deeply (3) and reinforces the feel you want on a sand shot.

Set some bunker guide sticks to help you with your sand play. One stick runs along the target line, while the second one runs in front of the feet, set open to the target line (1). The third stick is parallel to the second, just outside the ball (2). Notice how my feet are angled toward the target along with my open stance (3), and the ball position is center, not forward. On the backswing, the club moves

back parallel to the guide stick in front of your feet (4), not pulled back around the body so that the handle is pointing right of the target. You can see from this direction (5) how open my stance is—about 30 degrees—and how the club moves on a path across the ball (6). When you practice bunker shots, pick both your landing spot (7) and the eventual target to work on distance control and feel.

the clubhead dig too far into the sand. The ball pops right up and out of the bunker. As you continue to hit shots from the top of the rake, you'll automatically make some adjustments so that you don't bang the handle with the leading edge—the club will move easier along the top of the wood if the bounce is what's hitting it, not the edge.

You can use guide sticks in the bunker just as you did for your high shots, with some slight modifications. Start by laying one stick on a straight line to the hole. The second stick should approximate your open stance, and be aimed 30 degrees left of the target line, just in front of your toes. The third stick should be just outside the ball, parallel with your toe line. As with the high shot, your clubhead will be aimed straight at the hole—open in relation to your open stance—and you will swing the club on the same line as your feet. Take the club back so that it's parallel to the stick in front of your toes when the club is at waist height. From there, it will work on a vertical plane and cut across the ball at impact, producing height and spin.

After you've tried these drills, take a few balls and practice hitting to a target circle, just like you did on the high shots. That will help you work on your visualization and your distance and direction control.

Putting

I covered putting in great detail in my last book, *Unconscious Putting*, but I wanted to give you a couple of practice routines here to round out your short-game lesson.

The basic visual drill I use myself and that we teach in our clinics is the tee routine. When you visualize the path your ball will roll into the hole, you want to pick a very specific part of the hole where the ball will enter at the end of that path. When you pick that spot, stick a tee into the edge of the cup on the practice green, and then roll a few putts with the goal of bouncing the ball off that tee.

You can really work on your speed control with this drill, too. On shorter putts, stick the tee into the entry point of the cup, and practice rolling putts that die into the hole just short of the tee or curl in just above it. You get so engrossed in the game of missing the tee—or trying to kiss balls off the tee and drop them in—that you don't even feel like you're practicing. It's a game, and an addictive one.

We came up with a training aid specifically to help players do the basic

You should pick an exact entry point for every putt you hit. On the practice green, mark it with a tee (1), and practice rolling putts so that they hit the tee on the way to the hole (2). You can also buy training aids that create a gate on one side of the hole or the other (3).

things that we teach on the putting green: the Spot Putting Secret by Stockton Golf. When you place the t-shaped plastic trainer on the green, it has two tees that hold it in place at the target-side end, a small hole to set the ball on, and a white target dot. The goal is simple. Set up using the trainer as a guide, and see your ball roll over the white spot. If you set up the guide carefully so that it's aimed correctly, you can make strokes concentrating only on rolling the ball over the white target spot—and the ball will go on its way between the tee "goalposts" and into the hole. Actually, it almost doesn't matter if the ball goes in or not. What we're trying to establish here is that your primary focus when you set up to putt needs to be that aiming point in front of the ball. You've already done the work reading the putt and visualizing your line, and the only job you have now is to roll the ball over that spot. Then it's out of your hands. So many players struggle at impact with recoiling the putter, or consciously trying to hit at it, and this aid and drill really helps smooth that out.

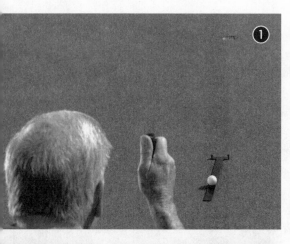

The Spot Putting Secret by Stockton Golf is a T-shaped guide that sets you up to roll the ball over your aiming point (1). Use the guide to align yourself and the putterhead (2), then roll the ball over your aiming spot. It helps you focus on keeping your eyes quiet and still.

NINE

Equipment

If you walk over to the wedge section of your local golf superstore, you'll see racks and racks of choices—both in terms of manufacturers, and the wide variety of wedges that each of those manufacturers make. TaylorMade's new line of variable-sole ATV wedges comes in seven different lofts, and Bob Vokey builds twenty-one different loft and bounce combinations for Titleist. Callaway and Cleveland also make terrific products. In fact, Roger Cleveland was a fraternity brother of mine at USC, and he was also in Cathy's and my wedding. It always amazes me how much he knows about wedges. First at Cleveland and then at Callaway, he's always been on the leading edge of wedge design.

That's a far cry from when I joined the tour in 1964. First off, the only loft option on a sand wedge was pretty much 56 degrees. If you were lucky enough to get an endorsement deal, you tried to sign one that gave you the option to pick your own wedges from any company. Because the reality then was that Spalding, Wilson, and Titleist were making the best wedges. But each of them were handmade, and you had to really search to find one that had the right shape on the sole and the right feel in your hands. Within the same model of wedge, you might try one and it would dig into the ground, while another one would slide through the turf. It was really important to find the right one, because you only had one wedge, and it had to be useful for a variety of different shots.

Today there are so many more options out there, with clubs designed to do just about anything you could want in the short game. You can get ones that will skid easily through sand, or glide through turf for easier shots from the fairway. You can even get one with 64 degrees of loft. Watching Phil Mickelson use his makes me wonder how he doesn't hit himself in the forehead when he plays a shot with it. He's an absolute surgeon with a lofted wedge around the green.

But with all the high-quality choices comes some more complicated decisions. Each wedge in your bag has to do what it's supposed to do for you and your swing, and they also have to work with each other and with the rest of the clubs in your set. But many players actually spend less time picking their wedges than they do their putter, driver, or even hybrid clubs.

I think that's a huge mistake.

You use your putter more than any other single club in your bag, but your short-game clubs come in close behind. You're going to use your favorite sand and chipping club—a 56-, 58-, or 60-degree wedge—at least a dozen times around the green during a round, and that doesn't count any full shots you hit with it from the fairway.

Why, then, are so many people content to just use the generic sand wedge that came with their set, or the basic 56-degree model they picked off the rack without too much thought?

I believe that wedges are specialty clubs just like the putter is. You can go out and buy a set of irons you like, and a set of fairway woods, and a set of hybrids. But when it comes to your wedges, you need to carefully choose which ones feel the best, and which mix of lofts and bounce angles solves all the problems you're trying to cover. That might mean that you buy a different brand of wedges than the rest of your set, or even wedges from two or three different manufacturers.

But once you find wedges that fit you and suit the shots you've learned to hit from this book, you're going to feel like you have some weapons in your hands. Good wedges are so easy to hit that they almost hit themselves. If you've learned the simple techniques from the previous chapters and you're still fighting your wedges, you need to make some changes.

Let's start by talking about what makes up the basic configuration of a wedge. The three main pieces are 1) the loft, 2) the shape of the sole, and 3) the swingweight. A wedge's loft basically determines the height of the shot it will produce relative to the other clubs in the set. Wedges come in virtually every loft from 48 to 64 degrees—with the higher number denoting a higher-launching shot. The loft number on the back of the club is one thing, but how it actually performs in real life is another. You can hit clubs built by different manufacturers that are technically the same loft, but the clubs can produce very different shots. The only thing that really matters is how the club performs in real life for you, measured by your eye and your club-fitter.

The second piece is the shape of the sole. Wedges are categorized by the bounce angle they have on the sole. Bounce angle is basically the amount, in degrees, that the trailing edge of the sole of the club drops down below the leading edge. A club with a high bounce angle of say, 12 degrees, has a trailing edge that hangs down much lower than a club with little or no bounce. That trailing amount of bounce acts as a skid, preventing the club from digging too far into the turf or sand.

Some people are obsessed with the amount of bounce on their club. I actually don't even know how much my wedges have. I'm much more

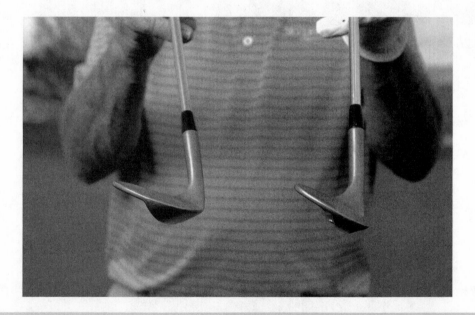

The triangle of metal on the back and bottom of the wedge is called the bounce. The amount it hangs down from the leading edge of the club is the bounce angle. My 60-degree wedge (left) has a more rounded sole with less bounce angle, while the 56-degree wedge (right) has a sharper, V-shaped sole with more bounce. Lob wedges range from 6 to 10 degrees of bounce angle, while 56-degree clubs usually have 10 to 12. The bounce angle number doesn't matter as much as how the club feels on your shots.

concerned with the shape of the sole, and how the wedges actually respond when they hit the sand or the turf. Back in the old days, I would hit my new wedges a bunch of times in practice and in tournament rounds and gradually wear away the material in the middle of the sole's bottom, so that the sole itself became concave. As the sole became more concave, the club performed better and better for me. I started looking for wedges that were already built with a concave sole, like the Spalding Dynamiter or the Wilson Staff wedges I used early in my career. When the ConSole wedges came out in the early 1970s with a radical version of that concave sole, they were

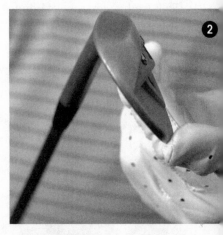

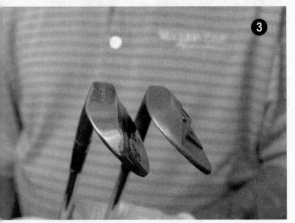

I've used a variety of wedges in my career (1), from the TaylorMade ZTP wedge in my bag now (left) back to the Wilson Staff (middle) and Spalding Dynamiter (right). The technology has improved over fifty years, but my preference in sole shape has stayed the same (2). I like the sole to have a concave shape—the leading edge and trailing edge are slightly raised, while the material on the flat part of the sole is slightly recessed. This gives the kind of contact with the sand and the turf that I'm looking for (3). You used to have to create this concave shape by hitting thousands of shots. Now you can buy wedges with the specific kind of grind you prefer.

extremely popular. When you use only the front edge and back edge of the bounce, it's much more effective from a variety of lies than a wedge with a lot of bounce right in the middle.

Instead of worrying too much about the bounce number on your wedge, go try some wedges with different sole configurations, and use them to hit all of the shots you play in your regular game. A good wedge needs to be able to produce full shots, low shots, high shots, and bunker shots all with the same grind on the sole. You might prefer a wedge with a more convex sole, or one that has more of a grind on the heel so that you can easily open the face and rest the club flat on the ground. It's absolutely a matter of personal preference and fit. Clubfitters have elaborate systems designed to measure exactly where the sole contacts the ground or the sand and where the ball contacts the face. A good fitter will be able to guide you into the right family of wedges for your type of technique.

The third piece of the wedge puzzle is swingweight. Swingweight is the measurement of "head heaviness" in relation to the grip of the club. If the club has a relatively high swingweight of D5, it means that the clubhead feels heavier in relation to the handle. Generally speaking, tour players prefer irons with lighter swingweights, like D2 or D3. But they're divided on their philosophy when it comes to wedge swingweights.

I have always preferred my wedges to have a heavier swingweight than the rest of my set. My irons have always been D2, while my wedges are D5. I want to be able to feel the clubhead swing, and I feel that the heavier head moves through the grass and sand with no extra effort. Some players prefer a lighter swingweight in their wedges, to the point where you'll see some of them with wedges that have holes drilled out of the sole material. I was working with Dustin Johnson recently, and I was surprised to find that his wedges were the same swingweight as his irons. He's a big, strong guy, so maybe all of his clubs would feel light to him anyway. But we changed the swingweight on his wedges to D7, and he said he immediately felt more comfortable with them.

I'm not saying either way is right or wrong. I just want you to be aware that there are more choices than just "stock," and to experiment to find the weight that feels good to you. You can even experiment with the clubs you already have by adding some sticky lead tape to the sole, on the back of the leading edge—away from the area that skids along the ground. The other ways to increase swingweight require more work—changing out the shaft or the grip to something lighter.

The grip you use on your wedges shouldn't get overlooked even if you aren't changing the swingweight of the club. A vast majority of players just grab a wedge off the rack and use it with the stock grip—and never change it for the entire life of the club. The wedges are scoring clubs just like the putter is, and you need to be just as conscious of the details on them.

I find that the stock grips on most wedges are too small for the average player—never mind the player who has hands that are larger than average. If you use a grip that's too small, you'll tend to squeeze the handle too tightly, which hurts your feel and restricts the natural release of the club. A larger grip lets you actually move the club. I use a size 58 round grip (with no built-in "reminder" pattern, unlike the grips on the rest of my irons) on my wedges, and I'll have two extra wraps of tape put on underneath. When we started working with European Tour player Nicolas Colsaerts, we had him add a full wrap under the length of the grip, and another wrap under his right hand.

Grip materials and textures come in hundreds of combinations—everything from super-soft and shock absorbing to firm and corded for more grip. Wrap-style grips simulate the feel of the old leather grips, while "velvet" grips have a more uniform, softer feel. Personally, I like a softer feel. I'm not as concerned about how durable the grip is, because I have the grips changed out every six months or so. A good golf shop will have lots of grips to sample. Just make sure you actually try them when they're on a real club—not just on one of the cutoff shafts. You want to be able to feel the grip when it has the full weight of a clubhead on the end of it.

Your wedges are in your hands more often than any other club except the putter, and like the putter, they need to have the grips changed a lot more often than the rest of the clubs do. If you're playing once a week and hitting balls another time or two, you need to change the grips on your wedges more than once a season, and change the grip on your putter three times. You can probably get away with changing the grip on your driver, woods, hybrids, and irons once a season, in the spring.

Believe it or not, players used to have to worry about wear on the grooves in the face of the wedge, especially if they played a lot of golf. The USGA didn't regulate groove depth the way they do now, and you could put a tremendous amount of spin on short shots with fresh, deep grooves. Players who hit a lot of shots actually wore the face of their wedge down in the center, where they made the most contact. It became a problem if you got really attached to one of your scoring clubs, because you had to basically throw the whole thing away at that point and hope you could find another with just the right combination of specs and feel. TaylorMade now makes a series of TP wedges that have detachable faces, which completely solves the problem. You can find a club that has just the right feel for you, and then simply pop a new face in when the old one wears out, or even change it for one with different playing characteristics if you're going to a place where you want to hit shots with more or less spin.

If you've gotten this far in the book, you've hopefully been able to work on the basic high and low shots we talked about, along with the bunker and trouble shots. But I also hope you've used the clubs that you already have to work on these shots, rather than simply going out and buying some new wedges. That's the right order to do it in—learn the shots, and then find the clubs to fit your body and the shots you want to hit. Once you know how to hit the shots, you'll be able to feel if the club isn't coming through the turf the way you like, or if you're not getting good spin out of the bunker. Then you can make your decisions on new clubs with complete information. If you do it the other way, and buy the clubs first, you're always going to be letting the club dictate the technique you use.

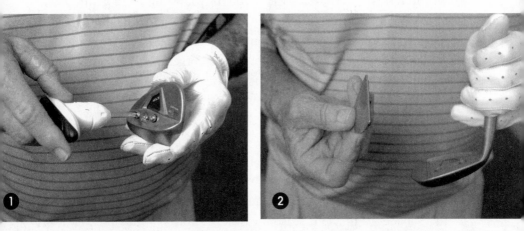

New wedge models from TaylorMade have faces that detach with two screws and a little wrench (1). When the grooves wear out, you just replace the face, not the entire wedge.

When you go to get fitted, you want to make sure to take the fitter through the most important shots you're going to hit—the low shot, the high shot, a couple of varieties of bunker shots, and full shots with each wedge. You're going to be able to hit the low shot with just about any wedge you pick, because most of the bounce on the sole is off the ground in the setup. The grind on the sole becomes more important as you hit high shots and bunker shots. You're going to want to feel how all the wedges move through the turf for high shots from fairway grass—make sure they don't dig—and to get a sense for how the club works through deeper rough grass. It's really important to hit both a 40-foot explosion shot out of the bunker and some longer bunker shots with the lower lofted wedges and see how the bounce on your sand club is interacting with the sand. I hit a lot of bunker shots with my 60-degree wedge, but that may or may not be something you choose to do. If you do, it's important to get a sense for how the bounce on any club you pick would work on that shot.

Assuming you've gotten pretty good with those shots, it's now time to make some decisions about your wedge lineup. The longest wedge in your bag, the pitching wedge, has to serve mainly as a club for full shots from the fairway and rough. So it's important that that club fits in with the tail end of your iron set in terms of carry distance. If you hit your 9-iron 125 yards, you're going to want a pitching wedge that flies at least 10–15 yards shorter.

How you configure the rest of your wedge set is partially determined by what the rest of your bag looks like. I'll never forget the conversation I had with Tom Kite after he had put the first 60-degree wedge on tour in play for a year or two. That wedge had already helped him win the 1990 U.S. Open at Pebble Beach, and we were talking about it not long after. I had played my entire career with one specialty wedge—a 56-degree. The rest of my set was pretty standard for the tour at that time—driver, 3- and 5-wood, 2-iron through 9-iron, pitching wedge, and putter.

Tom stopped me with a simple question. He asked me how many birdies I had made the previous season with my 2-iron. For him, the math was pretty simple. He had a much better chance to make more birdies and save more pars by having another wedge that he could hit both full from the fairway and rough and higher on trouble shots around the green than he did by hitting a long iron from 200 or 220 yards away. He bent his 3-iron a little stronger and choked down on his 5-wood for longer shots, and put the 2-iron away forever. It didn't take long to see that that was the way to go for me, too.

Now hybrid clubs make long shots so much easier for everybody—from tour players to 20-handicappers. It's easier to make the decision to drop a 2-iron, 3-iron and even a 4-iron from the bag for one or two hybrids. The number of long clubs you keep obviously determines how many scoring wedges you can use. I dropped both the 2-iron and 3-iron, and I have a 48-degree pitching wedge, a 54-degree gap wedge, and a 60-degree lob wedge. And my 4-iron has been replaced by a hybrid.

The key is to build out the set so that you cover the widest possible variety of both full and short shots. I hit my 48-degree pitching wedge 117 yards, and my 60-degree wedge 82. The 54-degree club I carry fits right in the gap, at 100 yards. If you went from a 52-degree wedge all the way up to a 60, you'd have 25 yards of carry difference between them, which is a lot for such short clubs. With a smaller gap between wedges, you're making full or near full swings on more shots, which are a lot easier to hit than 60 or 70 percent shots. At that point, you just have the distance you can get making a full swing with your most lofted club—in my case, the 60-degree from 82 yards—to the green to worry about contending with less than full shots.

The 60-degree isn't your only option for a higher-lofted club. If you're a strong person who puts a lot of spin on your iron shots, you can certainly choose a 52-degree gap wedge and a 58-degree lob wedge, and use the remaining club somewhere else in your set, like another long iron or hybrid. You've probably seen tour players like Phil Mickelson using 64-degree wedges, but those aren't something I'd recommend for anybody with higher than a scratch handicap. They're difficult to hit, and they don't offer that many more shots than a 60-degree—especially on golf courses that aren't set up super-hard like they are on tour.

One question I get from time to time is about the new grooves that manufacturers have had to use on their wedges since the USGA changed their spin rules at the beginning of 2011. Players want to know if they need to hoard old wedges with the sharper grooves, since anything made before the change is grandfathered in. I honestly don't see a lot of difference. You could spin the old wedges better, especially on full shots, but the manufacturers have basically just added more grooves and made the entire face rougher, so you can still spin the ball pretty well. The reality for most handicap players is that they're going to gain a lot more from the overall advances in the design of the latest wedges than they'll lose with grooves that are less sharp than they used to be. I bet if I blacked out the wedges and the balls and asked most non-tour players to pick out which wedges used the old grooves and which ones featured the new, most couldn't tell the difference.

The conversation about the type of ball a player uses pretty much follows the same thread. It used to make a much bigger difference than it does now. When I turned professional, you basically had the choice of a few different kinds of balata balls, and all of them spun a lot. As we went through the 1970s and 1980s, you could play a high-spinning tour balata ball, or a two-piece hard ball that didn't spin at all. Amateur players who used low-spinning balls really couldn't count on checking a shot up or spinning it much in any way.

But now, the average multilayer ball that the handicap player can get for $20 or $25 a dozen is remarkably good, and it both spins less on tee shots and more on shots around the green. And you can pick virtually any characteristic—more spin, less spin—you like. I would advocate choosing a ball that gives you the most control on tee shots but still feels relatively soft around the green. The techniques I showed you in the first few chapters aren't hugely reliant on spin, and you'll be able to put enough on any of the mid-level balls sold by the major manufacturers that it's something you're not really going to have to worry about.

The reality is that if you learn how to hit the shots and have confidence in your scoring game, you can use just about any ball or club that fits you.

TEN

Putting

There's no question that putting is a critical part of the short game. Just like with a good chip shot or bunker shot, you can cover up some serious mistakes by rolling in a 20- or 30-footer or two. I covered this subject in depth in my last book, *Unconscious Putting*, and if you read that one, most of what you're going to see here will be familiar.

But even if you know the stuff in the last book by heart, it will be worth your time to go through this chapter with me. Team Stockton helps more than two dozen tour players on every major tour, and I can tell you that Ron, Dave Jr., and I do more than just consult with a player once and then send them off into the world. Putting is all about feel and adjustments, and sometimes a player needs an outside set of eyes or to hear something that he or she already knows but got away from to feel things click back into place.

Plus, I'm going to talk about a couple of subjects in much more detail here than I did in *Unconscious Putting*—the importance of having both a physical and mental pre-shot routine, and what you should take away from the explosion in popularity of the belly putter on the professional tours.

Let me start by giving you an overview of my philosophy when it comes to putting. It's the only part of the game that a child can not only intuitively understand, but also do without any coaching beyond showing him which end of the club to hold. There are a few basic mechanical fundamentals that can make it easier to roll the ball without making a lot of physical compensations during the stroke, but even those aren't nearly as important as what I consider to be the art of putting: seeing the line, and then rolling the ball on that line.

Everything you do with a putter in your hand needs to be geared toward helping you see the line to the hole, and then setting up so that you can roll the ball down the line that you've visualized. It sounds very simple—and it is. But almost every player makes this child's game far more complicated than it has to be. It's not intentional. A lot of it comes from wanting to get better. A player will read a tip in a magazine or get a lesson from a teacher and start working really hard on making the "ideal" stroke. I used the example in the last book of signing your signature naturally, the way you would without even thinking about it, compared to trying to trace that first signature slowly. I want you to putt as though you're signing that first signature. When you think about mechanics, you let the stress and pressure of the situation out on the course get to you, or you get tentative because you've had a lot of bad experiences. In other words, you putt like you're tracing the second signature.

You need to be able to read it, see it, go through your routine, let it go, and just roll it.

Good putting comes from making a stroke like you'd write your signature. It's an unconscious move. Compare that feeling to trying to copy over your signature a second time, slowly. It's easier and more natural to make a stroke than it is to copy it.

What we're doing here is actually more unlearning than it is learning. I'm not going to give you a big laundry list of grip guidelines, stance rules, and stroke geometry to follow. I'm going to try to help you see the line more accurately and intuitively, feel more relaxed and free as you set up to the putt, and roll the ball on the line you see.

Let's start with the read.

Every putt you have is going to do something. Just what it's going to do depends mostly on the slope of the green, but also on the grain of the grass and even on the wind. I'm sure some of you are hoping to hear a scientific breakdown of how to determine the exact break a putt will have, but it doesn't work that way. I start by determining which way I think the ball will break—right to left or left to right. In fact, I never play any putt longer than four feet or so to roll straight in the hole. I always try to survey the area I'm putting in and make a call about a putt breaking one way or the other—even if it's very slight. Then I walk halfway between the ball and the hole to the low side of the break—the side opposite the apex of the putt's path—and

On each putt, find the apex of the break, then make your read from the low side—that is, opposite the side where the apex is. You can see much more of the break from that side.

study the putt from that angle. (I go to the low side because I think it provides the best angle to see the contours of the green. When you look downhill—from the high side—the perspective tends to flatten out.)

As I look at the putt from the low side, I see my line and then break it into thirds. The last third of the putt is where most of the action happens. As the ball is slowing down, it's going to take more break. I then visualize the line the ball will take to the hole—including the very specific part of the cup that the ball will enter. If the hole is represented by the numbers on a clock, I'll pick something like the five o'clock position for a putt that has a slight right-to-left break, or the three o'clock position for a putt with more break. Getting that specific about your entry point does two things. The more specific you are, the better and more effective your visualization of the line will be. And by picking an entry point in the cup instead of aiming for the middle every time, you give yourself more margin for error. If the only place the ball could enter was the six o'clock position, almost any putt hit a shade too hard or soft would miss. But if you pick the three o'clock position for a breaking putt, you can get away with hitting a putt slightly too hard and curling it in the top of the hole, or catching the lip and dropping in if you hit it a shade too soft.

How important is it to have a "perfect" line? Not nearly as important as having good speed control. You need to let go of the idea of being "perfect" when it comes to line, because you're playing on a natural surface with imperfections. You want to make the best read you can and trust it, and then roll your ball with good speed. My dad taught me to be "aggressive," in his terms, by setting me up with a breaking putt and putting one tee in the edge of the cup where the ball should roll in, and another one 18 inches behind the hole. My job was to practice kissing putts off the tee in the edge of the hole, but without leaving any misses either short or more than 18 inches past the hole.

Even if you completely stopped caring about direction and just improved your speed control so that you were no more than 18 inches past the hole, you would virtually never three-putt. It's almost impossible to misread a 15- or 20-footer by more than a foot or two. Get the speed right and you're going to have a lot of tap-ins. And once you start rolling the ball with good speed, you're going to get a good view of how much the ball breaks in that last third. And just seeing the ball roll over and over again is going to improve your innate ability to judge break.

The transition between read and stroke is where the problems really start for many players. The whole goal, as we discussed, is to translate what you see into where you actually roll the ball. Why, then, do most players lose that contact with the read by going through a bunch of practice strokes and staring down at the ball instead of where they want the ball to go?

My entire pre-putt routine is built to get me moving from my read to making my stroke in the minimum amount of time—all while staying connected to my line and keeping my thoughts simple and positive. You can have whatever kind of routine you like, as long as it's just that—a routine. That means it's something you do every single time. I'm in favor of a routine that's faster rather than slower, but if a slower one works for you, great. You just don't want to give yourself too much time to let negative or mechanical thoughts creep into your head.

A good routine is actually two routines—a physical one that includes your actual movement from the read into your setup, and a mental one that includes your thought processes. For my physical routine, I crouch behind the ball after making my read from the low side. After I confirm my read, I walk toward the ball, keeping my eyes focused on my line. When I'm a step or two from the ball, I'm looking at the last half of the putt. As I walk into my stance, I'm concentrating on the last foot of the putt (or the last few inches of a short putt), and I'm holding my putter in my left hand and making a few small practice strokes with my open right hand, for feel. I then step in with my right foot first, set my grip, and place my putter on the ground in front of the ball. Then I place my left foot while I'm looking at my entrance point to the hole. Then I bring the putter back over the ball. I look at the hole a second time, then my eyes come back to a spot an inch in front of the ball. Then I immediately make my stroke and watch the ball roll over that spot.

If you're wondering where a practice swing comes in, don't. It doesn't. I don't use one, and unless you absolutely need one to feel comfortable, I don't think you should use one either. It's a matter of staying connected to the line you see. When you take a practice stroke, you stand to the side of the line where you're actually going to play. When you do that, the tendency is to slide over into your stance in a position where you're aimed not on the line you saw but toward the hole itself. Even if you're able to move from your practice stroke into your stance and get yourself aligned to the ball the way you saw it in your read, your connection to that read isn't as fresh because you've been staring down at the club for five or six seconds. If you do have

After I make my read from the low side, I'll come back behind the ball and take one more look down low (1). After that, I move toward the ball while making small feel swings with my open right hand (2).

to use a practice stroke, do it the way Phil Mickelson or Annika Sorenstam does, perpendicular to the target line with your head up, before you start walking into the shot and going through your routine.

Even if you feel strongly that a practice stroke has to be a part of your routine, at least go out and try to play a couple of rounds without one. I think you'll be pleasantly surprised by what you learn.

My mental routine is just as efficient. It starts as I'm going through my read, where I reinforce my positive attitude. I approach every putt with the same mind-set: I can't wait to get up there and roll it, because I know I'm going to make it. Throughout my visualization process, I'm seeing the ball roll into the cup. As I walk into my stance, I'm concentrating on the line—not looking down at the ball—and I'm thinking two simple things. Back of the left hand to the target, and roll the ball over my spot.

Having a quiet mind—one that's focused on simple positive things—is the key to good putting. If you have a lot of mechanical thoughts running through your head, or you're worried about the consequences of missing, or you're tightening up because you feel like you "have to" make the putt, you're not playing with a quiet mind. You can test yourself by going out onto the practice green and rolling some putts out into the middle of it, without picking any target. When you do that, what did you think about? Your mind was probably blank. Compare that to your thought process when you have a short putt for birdie or to save an important par. You're close enough that it feels like you should make it, but far enough away that it's not a tap-in. That's when it starts to get a little noisier inside most players' heads.

The way you make your physical and mental pre-shot routines work for you is to impose them on every putt you roll—from the practice green to the 18th hole. Go through the same physical routine and use the same mental process for each one, and work on completing the routine in the same amount of time. Your goal is to keep the timing of when you start to step into your stance to when the ball leaves the putter the same, no matter what the situation. Just remember that slower is not necessarily better.

It's going to feel strange at first, going through the full routine on a practice putt all by yourself on the practice green, but after a short time—a week or two—you're going to notice that you've trained your brain in an interesting way. The routine will become a habit, and even on stressful putts out on the golf course, you'll find yourself automatically going through the routines you've been practicing, right down to the timing. That's an incredibly helpful, positive thing—almost a lifeline in a pressure situation. You can try to engross yourself in the process, and give yourself something to think about besides the pressure. The closer you can get to simply thinking about the back of your left hand moving toward the hole and trying to roll the ball over your spot—and forgetting about the outcome—the better the outcome is going to be.

I told a story in the last book about working with LPGA superstar Yani Tseng, and it's worth briefly retelling here, because it perfectly illustrates what I'm talking about. Yani was really struggling with her putting, and she called to see if I would meet her between events late in the 2009 season. She flew out to California and we got right into a cart and drove to the first tee. I asked her to hit a tee shot, and then an approach shot. For both, she took a couple of loose practice swings and ripped each shot. The tee shot went right down the middle, and the approach shot ended up five feet from the hole. But when we got to the green and I asked her to back the ball up and hit a 12-foot putt for me, everything changed. She got tentative and slow with her routine, and kept looking from her ball to the hole and back again. She didn't come

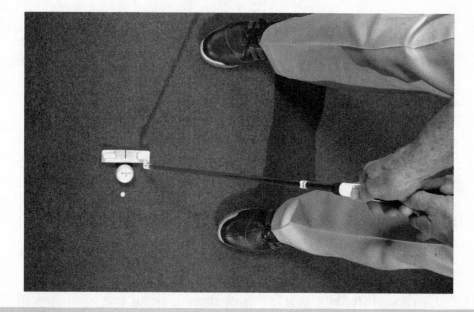

On your last look down before you roll your putt, don't focus on the ball, but on a spot just an inch in front of the ball. Then watch the ball roll over that spot.

close to making the putt. We made some simple changes to her routine to make it more consistent, and I asked her to make her read, trust it, and stand up there and let it go. We didn't change a single thing about her stroke. She won four majors and eight other tournaments over the next two seasons.

The subject of putting mechanics is a delicate one for me. I don't want to completely ignore it, because some players need some guidance about a more comfortable way to hold the club, or a stance that allows them to see the line more clearly. But I also don't want to put too much emphasis on it, because I truly believe that thinking more mechanical thoughts is just about the last thing any player needs—especially if you already roll the ball pretty well.

So what I'm going to do here is give you some general parameters that I use when I'm watching somebody putt—and I'll put a big qualifier on it. If you roll the ball well with the grip, stance, and setup you currently use, I'm perfectly OK with it. Watching Bobby Locke, Gary Player, Arnold Palmer, Jack Nicklaus, Loren Roberts, and me putt is to see six guys doing a lot of things differently. But we've all made miles of putts. I want you to use a grip and a stance that will help you roll the ball without thinking too much, and without having to manipulate the putterface through impact to send the ball on the line you see. You can use the technique descriptions here as a loose guide, and then mix and match them in a way that suits you.

Any swing in the game starts with the grip, and putting isn't an exception. As you'll hear in a second, I don't think you have to swing the putter in a certain way—on an arc or straight back and straight through. And I don't have a problem if you want to use an interlocking, overlapping, reverse-overlapping, or 10-finger grip when you putt. Any of those will work just fine as long as you keep a few things in mind. The first is balance. I like to see a neutral grip, where the back of the left hand is aimed directly at the target and represents the face of the putter, and the back of the right hand is parallel to that. When you turn your hands one way or the other on the grip, you have the potential to lose that balance. If you want the hands to work together to produce a simple, smooth putting stroke that doesn't require a lot of thought or manipulation, you need to start with a balanced grip. It's even OK to shift your hands on the grip, as long as you shift them the same amount, so that they oppose each other.

As far as grip placement goes, I want the back of the left hand to go to the hole in the stroke. To encourage that, the handle of the putter needs to run across your left palm and under the pad at the base of your left thumb. The pad of the right thumb rests on top of the left thumb, and you hold the handle in the fingers of your right hand. I spread my fingers slightly so I can feel a lot of the grip, but I don't extend my right index finger down the shaft, a move that tends to promote a hitting action instead of a smooth stroke.

I've always used a reverse-overlapping putting grip—the same one my dad taught me when I was a kid. The index finger of my left hand rests on top of my right hand, in between the knuckles of my pinky and ring fingers. I like this grip because it encourages me to move the back of my left hand toward the hole in the stroke, which is my major swing thought.

When I'm holding the handle of the putter, my grip pressure is extremely light—just enough to hold onto the grip so that it doesn't fall out of my hands. I feel the most pressure between the index finger and thumb of my right hand, and in the last three fingers of my left hand—especially in my overlapping finger. The feel in my fingers is very much like it would be if I was doing something delicate, like tying a fishing fly, or picking up something fragile from a table with my fingertips.

The left hand (1) sets up so that the back of it is facing the target, and the left thumb runs down the top of the shaft. The handle is running across my palm and under the pad at the base of my thumb. The right hand sets up parallel to the left (2), and I'm holding the shaft more in my fingers. When the hands come together on the shaft (3), they're facing each other, and the pad of the right thumb is resting on top of the left thumb. Your feel comes from your thumb and index finger. The middle and index fingers are loosely on the handle.

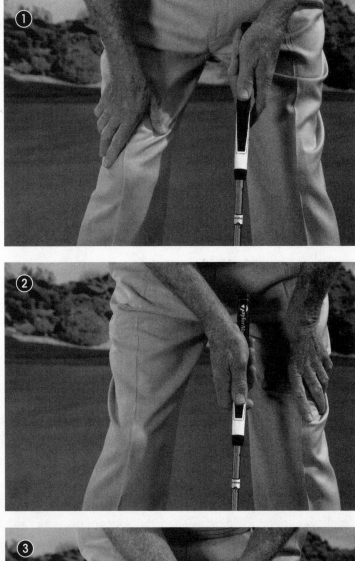

Grip pressure is so important to monitor both when you practice and when you play, because tension tends to make it increase. And when you tighten your hands, the muscles in your forearms and shoulders follow, and you start to restrict the natural movement of all those body parts. You want to feel loose and calm, to the point where the stroke feels as though it's just happening, that it's not getting pushed or pulled into motion. The putter-head will get to the back of your stroke and you'll be able to just let it go.

When it comes to stance, I think it's easier to see the line when your feet—not your shoulders—are slightly open. My left foot is an inch or two farther away from the target line than my right. I set my right foot first, then my left, and then I bend from my hips so that my arms can hang loosely near my sides. I'm not in a crouch, and I'm not standing upright. I would call it an athletic posture.

My stance width might get wider or narrower depending on what I'm seeing on any given putt, but my ball position—both along the target line and in terms of its distance from my feet—stays pretty consistent. I set up so that the ball is under my dominant eye—my right eye—which puts it just forward of the middle of my stance. I like the handle of the putter to be in a neutral position at address—in the position it would be if you just set the sole of the putter on the ground. This way, the handle ends up being

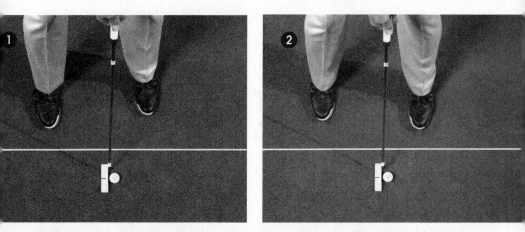

I like to set up with my stance slightly open relative to the target line (1) because it helps me see the line better. When you get closed (2), you have to manipulate your stroke too much, and it becomes more of a conscious move instead of a reaction.

You want to be in an athletic position, with your weight on the balls of your feet and the ball underneath your dominant eye. That's usually just forward of middle in the stance. It's less important how far apart your feet are, as long as your ball position stays consistent.

parallel to your zipper, and your hands aren't lifted or pushed down unnaturally. If your hands are lowered from neutral at address, they'll have a tendency to get too active during the stroke. The higher the hands get, the more the left hand controls the stroke, and the quieter the stroke gets. Lower hands tend to cause misses to the left, while higher hands produce a miss to the right.

As I said before, my basic swing thought is to take the back of my left hand toward the hole. When I do that, the putter stays low and along the target line right through to my finish. I start my stroke with a slight forward press—a shifting of the handle toward the target—to begin from something flowing rather than from a frozen, still position. I make a slight shift of the handle a couple of inches toward the hole, and as soon as that motion starts, my left index finger triggers the movement of the putterhead into the backswing.

People ask me all the time if I swing the putter on an arc or straight back and straight through, but to be honest, I don't ever think about that. Once I trigger my stroke, I just let it go, without consciously thinking about making the head go inside, straight, or outside. Honestly, I don't think it really matters, as long as the face is relatively square when it meets the ball.

If you find that some of these "conventional" ideas aren't working for you, you do have some other choices. I like to roll the ball off the face of the putter in a smooth motion. When the right hand gets active and releases through impact, it produces more of a hit—something that makes distance control more difficult. It's a common problem for players who have the yips. In that case, a cross-handed or saw grip can be helpful.

In a cross-handed grip, you simply change the positions of the right and left hands on the handle. The backs of the hands still oppose each other, and the back of the left hand is still pointing straight at the target. It just changes the relationship between the hands and lets the left hand control the stroke. The saw grip serves the same purpose. In that one, the player keeps his left hand on the grip in the same way, but rotates the right hand off the handle so that the side of the palm rests along the side of the handle to guide it. It takes the hinge out of the top of the right wrist, and basically makes the right hand a quiet extension of the right arm. It's just along for the ride.

Alternative grips have gotten a fair amount of play on the PGA Tour over the last twenty years—Jim Furyk was Player of the Year with a cross-handed grip, and Bernhard Langer has won events on both the PGA Tour and the Champions Tour with a variety of different grips and a variety of different-length putters. But the biggest recent story in putting has been the explosion in the number of players using a belly putter. Angel Cabrera used one to win the Masters in 2009, but it was the procession of wins with the longer club in 2011 that really sparked the trend. Adam Scott, Webb Simpson, and Keegan Bradley all won with belly putters, and Bradley's win came at the PGA Championship, which gave the belly putter a lot more exposure.

But the most attention probably came from a guy who didn't win with one, and didn't even use it for very long. Phil Mickelson played a practice round with Bradley after the PGA and asked him some questions about the club. Bradley had a lot to say about it, and Phil is always open to experimenting with anything he thinks will make him play better. So when he put the putter in play at the Deutsche Bank in September, my phone went nuts. After that, I had TaylorMade make me a couple of them so I could get an idea about how they worked.

There's no question that it felt foreign to use one, but I can see why players like them—even if it's hard to understand how the USGA ever made them legal. The club is anchored in your belly, and all you're left to do is move your hands back and forth. I'm sure it makes the stroke feel very stable and repeatable for guys who struggle with that. The anchored handle basically works to control the arc from a fixed point.

When long-handled putters came out twenty years ago, they were generally considered to be crutches for players who had completely lost their putting stroke, or had the yips—guys like Bruce Lietzke and Orville Moody. They never got much more than fringe acceptance, even on the Champions

I set my stance while I'm looking at the target and the putter is in front of the ball (1). While still looking at my target, I set my feet (2), then move the putter back behind the ball and look down at the spot in front of the ball (3). The stroke starts with a slight forward press, shifting the handle toward the target (4).

My left index finger triggers the putter moving back (5), and my only thought as I roll the putt is the back of my left hand going to the hole (6).

Tour. But now you're starting to see guys who can putt very well with the short putter—like Phil Mickelson, who went back to the regular putter at his next event, the Presidents Cup in Australia, and went on to win again early in 2012 with his blade—picking it up because they see that they get an advantage. The stigma is off, and I think you'll see a ton of younger players trying them. It's all about making more birdies.

It puts the USGA in a tough position. The belly putter has undoubtedly kept some players competitive who otherwise wouldn't be. How do you tell Fred Couples he can't use one? He wouldn't play. And I've read that sales of belly putters were up 400 percent in 2011 over the year before, with projections for 2012 even higher. Are you going to take that club out of tens of thousands of average players' hands? I think the horse might be out of the barn when it comes to making them illegal.

If belly putters are here to stay, does it make sense for you to try them?

Sure. If you don't feel like your stroke is consistent, a belly putter could definitely help you. The core of what I teach—seeing the line, having a routine, and rolling the ball on your line—work the same whether you're using a standard putter, a belly putter, or a shovel. If you do try one, let me give you a few tips that will make the transition smoother. The conventional place to anchor the belly putter is square in the middle, near your belly button, but I've found that moving the anchor point forward a couple of inches, toward the hole (in other words, a couple of inches to the left for a right-handed golfer), allows the putter to release and stay lower along the target line. I got a better roll that way. You also want to make sure that the club has enough loft—something between 2.5 and 3 degrees is ideal. Length is also extremely important. If it's even a quarter of an inch off, you're going to struggle.

When we run putting clinics, a lot of players will come up before we start and ask if what we teach will work better with a face-balanced putter or one that wants to work on more of an arc. Honestly, I don't think it matters, as long as the putter physically fits you, and you like the way it feels. I don't consciously

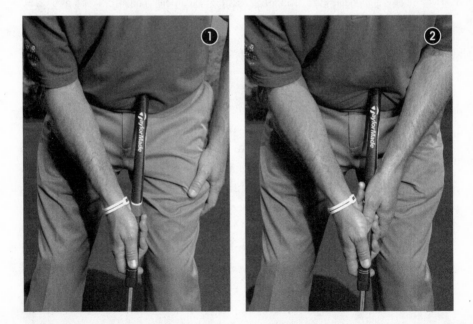

Your grip on a belly putter is the same as it would be on a standard putter (1). The right and left hands should oppose each other, and the back of the left hand should be aimed at the hole (2).

Some players anchor the belly putter in the middle of the gut, right at the belly button (1). To me, this causes the putter to release more up instead of toward the target. I get better feel if I anchor the putter two inches forward, toward the target (2). This will let you keep a slightly more traditional finish. It's really a matter of feel, though.

From down the line (1), it's hard to tell you're even using a longer putter. Be sure to get a long enough club so that you aren't too hunched over in your setup. Players like the belly putter because the anchor keeps the pendulum at a fixed point (2). You'll have to practice with it to get some feel on longer putts.

A cross-handed grip works the same on a belly putter as it does on a conventional one. The left hand takes the lower position, while the right hand moves above it on the handle. This reduces the movement of the right hand in the stroke.

think about the shape of my stroke—straight back and straight through or arc—and I don't think you should either. A certain flavor of putter is probably going to appeal to you more than others—say a mallet head versus an Anser-style blade—but there's nothing to say you can't mix and match over time. I've won tournaments with a variety of head shapes, but every one of the putters I've used in tournament play has had a similar feel and swingweight. Use what looks good to your eye and feels good when you roll it.

And don't forget to take good care of your equipment. Take care of your putter and it will take care of you.

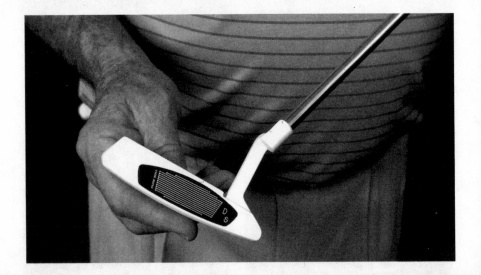

Picking a putter is totally about feel, but it's important that the club fits you. New face inserts improve the quality of the roll you get by making the ball come off with less skidding.

ACKNOWLEDGMENTS

Unconscious Scoring is the product of a lifetime of help from a lot of people, and I'm grateful for every one of them.

It started with the instruction I got from my dad, Gail Stockton, when I was a young player in San Bernardino, California. And it continued when I got out on tour, where I learned firsthand from some of the greats—Dale Douglass, Julius Boros, Lee Trevino, Don January, Hubert Green, and Gary Player. They opened my eyes to just how good a short game could be—and needed to be—to be a champion. There were many times when they could have given the new guy the cold shoulder and let me struggle, but they didn't. They were all extremely generous with their time and insight, and I'm a better player and teacher today because of it.

I'm very fortunate to be able to spend time helping some of today's generation of short-game artists, and I'm learning from them as well—players like Phil Mickelson and Rory McIlroy. You hear some older players say that there's not much touch and feel out on the tour anymore, but I just don't buy that. It's truly amazing how talented the best players in the world are today, and I'm convinced they would be champions in any era. It's been a special treat to spend time with Phil over the last few years and see how inquisitive he is about the game and how open he is to learning and trying new things.

It has always been an honor to represent the PGA of America, and I'm extremely thankful for the faith they showed in me when they made me Ryder Cup Captain in 1991. Winning two PGA Championships and leading those men at Kiawah are the highlights of my career.

It has been a pleasure to collaborate with my sons, Dave Jr. and Ron, helping tour players and amateurs around the world representing Stockton Golf. I can see my father in them through their teaching, and that is an amazing thing. Gail Stockton was the start, and the boys have taken what he taught to a whole other level. I couldn't be prouder.

My agent, Ralph Cross, has been a friend and trusted adviser throughout my career, and he was instrumental in what you're holding in your hands—as was Matt Rudy, my collaborator. I know how much goes into organizing and producing a book like this, but with Matt it never feels like work. He's the best. J. D. Cuban's photographs are fantastic, as usual. Scott Waxman and Farley Chase got us a great deal with Gotham, where Travers Johnson was on top of all the details.

Saving the best for last, my wife, Catherine, has been the ultimate partner and best friend for more than forty-seven years. I truly couldn't have done any of this without her.